The Myth of the Computer

BY THE SAME AUTHOR

Installing and managing a computer (*Rothery*)

The art of systems analysis
(*Byrne, Mullally and Rothery; edited by Rothery*)

The practice of systems analysis (*Rothery and Mullally*)

Brian Rothery

The Myth of the Computer

Business Books Limited *London*

First published 1971

ISBN 0 220 66816 7

This book has been set in 11 point Baskerville and printed in Great Britain by C. Tinling & Co. Ltd., London and Prescot for the publishers, Business Books Limited (registered office: 180 Fleet Street, London EC4), publishing office: Mercury House, Waterloo Road, London SE1

MADE AND PRINTED IN GREAT BRITAIN

Contents

Acknowledgement

I wish to thank my colleagues and Manager in CIE, the Irish National Transport Board, who were broad-minded enough to let me write this book while working with them, and who know that the issues considered here are international rather than local.

1 *the computer industry*

Why do managers get computers for their companies? The usual reason given is that real savings and efficiency can be achieved only by investing in computer techniques and technology . . . 'The knell has sounded for the clerk, and the computer is here to stay. . . .' and . . . 'Only by spending a lot of money and time on a computer in one's own company can one learn about how the computer can be used *properly* to one's advantage.'

This theme is taken up by famous professional computer advisers all over the world. Managers flock to see them, packing lecture halls in London and New York. Always the same stern message is hammered home—'more than half', 'more than 60 per cent' and, in some cases, 'more than 80 per cent of all computer installations are failures'. The managers listen enraptured, and one begins to wonder which interests them most, their own failed computer installation, or the idea that one of themselves, now a millionaire is up on the dais telling the rest how it should be done.

Management involvement, is the stern indictment from the advisers. 'Most computer installations fail because top-management are not involved.' True, but is it the whole story? Top management can be inept, but they can also be busy. How competent are these computer people who are riding on a tide of success in the modern world? It is easy to blame top management, but is it possible that the computer people themselves are sometimes at fault?

Why did these computer managers advise their companies to get computers in the first place? Perhaps it was because they had gone through a thorough cost-benefit analysis in which long-term and short-term systems plans were related to available computer hardware. And perhaps it was not.

Maybe it was for one of two other reasons, well-known, but never talked about in the computer industry. The first is prestige, often called power, the second is incompetence.

Knowing that to use such words amounts to treason in the computer industry, I must now say that some of the finest and most intelligent minds I know work with computers. These people, however, do not buy computers for industry; they are hired to instal and supervise the computers bought by others. Generally then, when I talk about incompetence or even dishonesty in this book, I am not talking about the technical computer people, a breed for whom I have the highest admiration; I am talking about managers who know nothing about the computer operations they are supposed to control, and about their managers in turn.

And knowing also that to use such words is to bite the hand that feeds, I must add that only one who has done well in the computer industry, and in many cases done well out of the kind of wasteful computer operation I will be talking about, is in a position to be critical. Excuses for being critical after some success are chiefly two: the first that most computer specialists work up from the bottom, from programmer usually, so that only at the top can they see projects in terms of economic viability, and only at the top can they see the real meaning of management; the second is the obvious excuse that one can be critical only when one can afford the independence of criticism.

One of the main problems to be faced in passing judgment on computer operations and computer managers is that the moment the word 'computer' is mentioned we step into a mythological world as powerful as surrounded Homer and his ancestors. There is meaning and power and even a sense of 'being' attributed to the technology, in general and particularly, the computer. Programmers unhesitatingly attribute 'mind' to the computer. 'I tried it with the library keyword, but it threw it out', they will say, adding things like, 'There is something in that code that it doesn't like'. They know well that all they are talking about is an electronic control program that is residing, for as long as the power is switched on, inside the 'hardware' of the computer. They do not really think it is a mind, but, and here is the rub, they find that the most convenient way to think about it, and to discuss it, is as if it were a being with a mind.

The reason for this is simple. The computer is the super machine, without a doubt, the nearest thing to an imitation of man's intelligence and by far faster than any man or group of men at routine work. It is admired and loved by the few who understand it, feared somewhat and respected by the fewer who use it to boost their prestige and power, and often hated by the mass of people who do not understand it at all.

It was interesting to note how public jokes about computers died away after the moon shots. Up to that time, they were abundant, first and secondhand accounts of the terribly stupid things that some computer had done, believed passionately by their storytellers who simply wanted to spirit the computer out of their particular portion of the mythological environment. Then the most fantastic computer-based acrobatic stunts the world had ever seen took place, men circling the moon, landing on it, getting off it again. The jokes about computers died away. It seemed they did work. There was, therefore, a more awful possibility, better not thought about. Perhaps *people* were behind computer troubles, not the computers themselves.

With nearly everyone wanting to climb onto the computer bandwagon, and an almost complete absence of informed critics, the computer mystic strengthens as the industry expands at what can only be described as enormous growth rates.

Right at the centre of the industry is the hardware, the centre of which is the computer itself, its importance reflected by the fortunes of IBM, fast becoming one of the biggest companies in the world, and certainly the company with the greatest image in the world. Even if a nitwit were hired by mistake into IBM, which is a most unlikely occurrence, he would begin to feel intelligent and perhaps would even act intelligently after awhile.

Interwoven with this hardware business is the altogether extraordinary 'software' business, in which fortunes can be made and lost. This loose term covers systems, programming, and operating or control systems and programs, and various packages or routines that help computer users to increase efficiency and to reduce their own programming load. Some of the fastest–richest men in history have emerged here in the last few years. Extraordinary success stories abound, reminiscent of the Klondike, of men starting off in single rooms with pencils and pads as their only capital equipment, making take-over bids for some of the world's largest utilities after a mere six years. These are the new technologist entrepreneurs, taking over from the owners of capital, who formerly displaced the owners of land. These are the undisputed heroes of the computer industry.

Then there are the education-mongers, ranging from the unsavoury night-school operators who exploit the hopes of the unendowed through promises of glamorous programming careers, to the seminar producers, text-book writers and, like this one, advisers, who, hopefully at least, exploit only an aware and educated minority who can afford it.

Beside them are the consultants doing an enormous business in telling computer users for thousands of dollars what they could usually have read in a textbook for a few, and telling top management what only an outside consultant dare tell them—that they are not competent to have a computer. (Which is perhaps worth the thousands of dollars fee.)

Next, the accessory suppliers, selling paper, cards, disk packs, tapes, furniture and cabinets, in what must be one of the most liberal and aggressive selling environments in the world. Much of what they sell, such as cards, disks and tapes can be bought from the supplier of the computer hardware, but despite this, business is very good. One reason for this is that users tend to avoid giving all their business to the computer supplier, on the assumption that he will give better service if something is withheld.

Then there are the hardworked service bureaus, selling computer time, data preparation, data communications or scanning. These range from the local three-in-a-back-room operation to huge international time-sharing information utilities.

We also have the computer user staff, the most precious and sought after of which, for the moment anyway, is the programmer. So exalted is he these days that entire weekly magazines and newspapers have come into being based on him and on his job mobility. These magazines reach him free of charge, paid for by the advertisers who wish to reach him and cajole him into joining their computer operations, or to let his name be placed on their job-placement lists. Flattered by his magazines and newspapers, deferred to by his senior analysts and systems managers, who need him as the most basic element in the maintenance of their own jobs, he has become confident to the point where he holds both management and unions alike in contempt. His one loyalty is given, unquestioningly, to the force that has made him—the computer industry.

More mature, and somewhat less confident than the programmer, although better paid, is the systems manager or data processing manager. The facts are crude but plain: although he may be the key person in the success or failure of a computer project, he is cosseted less than his programmers, for he can be more easily replaced—or so it appears to management at a glance. Only in this much maligned and seldom praised job is a computer man given the chance to be either hero or chief villain. There are exceptional cases where he is sat upon from above, but, generally, the basis for the success or failure of a project is laid here. A computer project can fail for many reasons beyond the data processing manager's control, but without his active interest it can never succeed.

And ignored until now on our financial and prestige chart,

and deliberately placed last and least at the end of the computer industry bandwagon, is the user. Who is he, we may well ask? Who is he, all those who have passed already and are making fortunes out of him may ask in turn. He is the poor devil who is paying for the computer revolution.

2 *the reasons behind the decision*

And so, says the company public relations man, our company must go forward with the rest of the world and move into the computer age. The computer is expected to bring increased savings and efficiency in the areas where it is to be first employed.

First of all, it is important to appreciate that the man who chooses the computer may not run the company, and that the man who runs the company may have neither the time, nor the training, to understand the meaning of a computer.

Take the expression above, repeated often in computer announcements: 'increased savings and efficiency'. Apart from the uncertain meaning and general nature of these words, are they as important as they are claimed so be? One needs savings and increased efficiency, but one could both save money and increase efficiency while working on a program that reduces sales and eventually brings a company to a halt. A certain kind of person will see things in terms of increased savings and efficiency, another will see as first priorities the objectives of increased revenue, stability in a market or environment.

Why, then, do we hear so much of the first two, which are conservative and reactionary? Because the clerk says them; whether he be accountant, secretary, engineer or management scientist, he is a person who sees things in terms of costs to be reduced and not more business or different business, but more efficient work. A most commendable attitude, compatible with punctuality and clean shoes, but a dangerous attitude in approaching a computer. The computer may not save any staff and it may not make some jobs more efficient. It may appear to offer both benefits, but may in fact be more expensive and less efficient than the way the job is now done.

Why, then, do apparently intelligent managers, especially accountants who are usually so careful, make decisions that are evidently based on something different than the cold facts? Without being too unkind, there are two possible reasons for the wrong decisions. One is simply old-fashioned incompetence. The decision, first to get a computer, then to pick the right computer, is enormously complicated. It takes experience and a lot of hard work. This would excuse certain failures where, for example, a computer turns out to be not quite big enough, but what about the situation where it is obvious that the company has been landed with an expensive sledgehammer that the job could never have justified and that costs are soaring? Here it will probably be found that the manager who decided in favour of the computer was incompetent, perhaps because of overwork or some job pressure, or simply due to his own personal inadequacies, which are sometimes just disinterest or laziness. Who sold it to him? A computer salesman who is on quota and under extraordinary pressure to sell. What about him? Is he not responsible for a share of the blame?

To answer that, let us assume that we are an unlucky manager who has been sold something that does not fit the job. Would we go to our general manager and tell him that we had been misled, saying that the computer salesman had told us a lie and not kept his promises? If we did, the general manager would deal directly with the unscrupulous salesman, but he would justifiably fire us first.

No one likes to cast the first stone in the second case, where the manager wants prestige through his association with a computer, but this can be a very important element in the decision to buy a computer, and one that the computer salesman is well aware of.

One of the first threats that the salesman makes to the hesitating manager is, 'If you don't decide quickly, and take the initiative, I'll guarantee that another department will have a computer installed before you know what has happened'. It is pretty plain: what he is saying is that here is your chance as an ordinary manager to get on the computer bandwagon, to achieve respect and power within your own organisation and to become a member of the exalted computer industry.

It would take more than a mere man to resist such temptation, especially faced with such vague possibilities as 'future savings'. Get it in now, the salesman urges. Get the bread and butter work onto it, and then when you have the know-how you can go on to bigger things. It is a Cinderella story, of course, for the bread and butter things may exhaust your hardware capacity, giving no savings, and leaving no room for bigger things. The bigger things the salesman had in mind may have been more expensive hardware.

There is even a kind of manager who wants it all ways. He wants the manufacturer to take the responsibility and expects the rewards to come to him. There is about one in every dozen at seminars for trainee data processing managers. When some rough speaker gives the facts, mentioning such things as not to expect too much support from the manufacturer after the machine is installed, other than the usual excellent engineering maintenance, and particularly not to expect the system to perform as the proposal said it would perform, he will protest that the manufacturer will therefore be legally in default.

The lecturer, amused at this, points out that the proposal was written for a given set of conditions at a given time. This means that the customer must build a system exactly as the manufacturer proposed it, for it to be the same. But the general nature of the proposal makes this impossible. Not only must all the variable things take place as stated for the comparisons of proposal with reality to be valid, but it must also be assumed that the customer programmed the job in whatever way the proposal intended. The computer manufacturer could reasonably argue that it could have been programmed in a way that realised the performance expectations set out in the proposal.

The vexed manager at this stage begins to argue back that such behaviour is not moral or ethical and that no reputable company could operate like that. The manufacturer must honour his guarantee to support the customer and to see to it that expectations are realised. If such arguments continue, the lecturer must point out to this would-be data processing manager that if the manufacturers loan a man to his company to do what he is asking, presuming they had one to spare, in other words to do his job, his boss will be so impressed by this help that he will hire the helper and get rid of him.

The message is plain. Once you rent or buy a computer, you are absolutely on your own. There is no situation so confused as one in which a computer is failing or not paying its way—the first to get hurt is the man in charge of it. There is no sense in looking for an arbitrator, for, apart from specialist consultants, no one will be in a position to understand or appreciate what has been going on, and even with consultants he may not get an unbiased opinion as we will see later.

If a decision to get a computer stems from reasons of incompetence or empire-building, why is it not always stopped higher up? One reason is that there is often even less understanding and greater incompetence higher up. This may seem harsh, and yet it is only a recent judgment from a systems man who has been examining the problems of management for some years. It was formed finally after seeing how certain presidents and directors, who take time out to tend to minute details that could be delegated, will sanction a decision to rent computer hardware worth a million dollars a year without blinking. One cannot blame certain other writers for concluding that such executives spend time only on the small things because this is all they understand.

Before attempting to suggest antidotes, it might be as well to state here what may not be obvious. This is not an anti-computer book or a negative approach to computers. The writer has already toiled through three very pro-computer works (*Installing and managing a computer*, Brandon Press, Business Books; *The art of systems analysis*, Prentice-Hall, Business Books; *The practice of systems analysis*, Business Books), but until now has never written about those areas that could not be quantified in systems analysis terms. The other books begin on the assumption that if you have some kind of policy directive to install a computer and do some systems work, here is how to go about it. Increasingly, as the books were written, it became apparent that their contents were only theoretical if management was not involved. And yet, they had to be written as they were, taking over from the point of the directive from above, for that is where the work of the computer man begins.

There are many also who operate with no directives, or bad directives, waiting for the day the axe will fall upon them for the inevitable questions of how much is it costing, and how much is it saving?

If his true answer is that not only is it costing more than the proposal said it should, and that not only is it losing money for the company instead of saving it, but that in addition he needs more people and hardware just to carry on the job as it is, then he may receive some comfort from this book, and indeed he may even be able to quote it to his general manager.

3 *the building of the myth*

The best time is in the beginning. Ask any old-timer of eight or ten years' experience who has been on several computer projects and he will agree that there is no time like it. No matter how sophisticated the hardware, the time will come when it becomes a mere data-processing operation with uniformed female operators carrying about data and files. But at the beginning there is the moment of pure creativity when a few people gather together in rented rooms with blackboards and scratch pads to plan. Within a couple of years a new building fully staffed and housing the hardware will come into being; meanwhile, the material out of which all is to be created is still in the mind.

Again, there are many ways in which they may go about the planning, some sensible and intelligent, others downright muddling. We will be trying to look at some of the sensible ways later, so meanwhile we will look at those that drift rather than follow a planned course.

Too often the whole project starts at the mythological level and stays there until the day of reckoning. The very first newspaper advertisements for the project leader sets the tone:

> 'The company intends to install a highly sophisticated computer system with data transmission links and real-

time facilities. The company, a leader in its field, already employs advanced MIS (management information system) concepts.'

Many of the revered words are already there in the advertisement. After much sweat, loss of sleep, and much money, it will be found that no matter how sophisticated the company and the computer hardware, it is simple arithmetic that decides whether the new system is running at a profit or a loss; in the first rush of enthusiasm, however, there is no time for such thoughts.

Much good can come from this enthusiasm in the early stages in those projects where the company stands to benefit from the installation of a computer, for morale and productivity are high. This comes about through the drafting into the computer staff of trainee programmers, often from within the organisation. These people, fired with enthusiasm for their new careers, apply themselves with such energy to the job that productivity levels rise to points that are not likely to be repeated. The wise manager takes advantage of this and tries to meet his all-important first target dates before the inevitable productivity decline.

Enthusiasm sustains the myth engendered in this early stage, for during that time everyone in the computer department believes strongly in the computer, even though only a few, or even none, may have seen a feasibility report. The critics are easily overcome by intelligent senior systems analysts, who, with their trained approach and logical minds, explode the arguments and expose their critics as reactionary.

On the side of the computer systems man is the modern philosophy of change. Change is good, for without change we become extinct like the dinosaur. Eighty-five per cent of the products that will be sold by the X Corporation in ten years have not yet come off the drawing board, and the computer is the chief agent of change.

It is all reasonably true with some major exceptions. The trouble is that one only finds the reactionary people opposing the computer, and invariably the opposition stems from such reasons as the fear of losing power or status. Invariably the intelligent man makes an intellectual and emotional decision not to fight change, but to embrace it and go forward with it, thus compounding the myth and playing into the computer salesman's hands.

What is truly ironical about this whole philosophy of change is that the computer, definitely the agent of change, may also be the agent through which a new era of permanence could be brought about. Of all devices, the computer could best support a semi-automatic world of balanced environment and little change.

The real strength of the computer group at this planning stage is the impending arrival of the computer, a key date on the critical path schedule. Decisions which would never be made without such a bulldozer on the horizon are made when the systems analysts simply point to the arrival date on the calendar and warn, that 'the computer is coming on that date'. After the computer arrives they may never again reach such a position of authority, and may find great difficulty in obtaining directives for, or support in, new systems.

This is also the stage where a badly informed top-management can be exposed to the grand illusions of the MIS, referred to, almost invariably in terms of hardware, an illusion sustained by the best known computer advisers. Terminal screens on the desks of the executives, hooked up by data transmission lines to the central computer complex in real-time mode. All information will be accessible immediately at the touch of a finger. Models can be manipulated by attached light pens right on the cathode ray screen of the terminal, so that possible courses of action can be simulated and results seen. What is often overlooked is what *information* will be in the MIS and how will it be gathered, manipulated and analysed.

The new computer staff support the myth of the omnipotence of the new system, not only by propagating the faith but by their very style. To user management, to whom they are a power that may drastically change their lives, they emanate intelligence. They can talk not only about the new hardware and software, but also about the company's information in new terms. One of their most dangerous weapons against anyone who resists is to talk about his job in front of his boss in such a way that they appear to know more about it than he does. Many a reckless manager has regretted having had a go at the computer staff at his first meeting.

A common situation is where a hard works manager, say, hearing complaints about the coming computer system from his chief clerks, goes along to the first group meeting that is attended by the assistant vice-president to whom he and the computer staff report. Unknown to himself, not having bothered to meet the computer staff on his own first, he is about to do battle, totally unprepared for what is to come.

If he is the old-fashioned storming type, he will not be able to wait too long after the meeting has started to fire the first round the way he has been doing for years, at his staff, suppliers, and union officials. His supporters will jump in on cue and air all their grievances. From the moment he has begun, the works manager will sense a difference. Either his arguments will be tactfully and intelligently taken to pieces in front of his superior by the senior computer man, who will disclose things about his job that he did not know existed, or he will be treated with amused contempt.

There are at least two very good reasons why the computer man manages to make such a good show when talking about someone else's job. The first is that he is trained to think in abstractions about abstract systems. The second is that people generally do not think about their own jobs beyond what they have to think. This is particularly true about an operating type of job where a manager is geared to action rather than paperwork. He simply has no time to think about how the information he needs could be improved. It is even true, however, of the accountant or clerk, especially when he has reached the stage where he no longer questions his own job. One could almost say that anyone with intelligence can make intelligent suggestions about another's job. How much easier it is, then, for a systems analyst, trained in information-flow and decision-making techniques.

When we add to this ability to talk about another man's job, the computer technology jargon and the brilliant concepts of MIS, the computer man attains awesome proportions. Fortunately for the thinking manager, the proportions are far from genuine. With few exceptions, computer systems analysts and programmers know very little about anything beyond their own limited knowledge of hardware and software.

Let us start with the much-sought-after programmer. He is good at his job, and he requires a certain valuable mentality that could be put to excellent use in many kinds of work from computers to criminal detection. He knows how to express a problem and how to go about solving it. But his is a most mundane job. He is a mere translator. He takes a system as expressed by the systems analyst and translates it into computer terms, so that the computer can run it. As a programmer what he does not know would fill books. The same is true of most systems analysts, who, to a great extent, are just promoted programmers. They take systems and, making a few adjustments perhaps, adjust them so that they can be run on the computer.

What is missing? Everything that matters. Most programmers, analysts and systems managers are only computer implementers. Left out are the systems analysts who understand the meaning of *information systems*, who understand the meaning of a *control system*, who know that only some of management's information is *quantitative*, the rest being *qualitative* and not easily expressed in data terms, who know that enterprises are steered as much with 'once-off' *adaptive* type information as they are with the recurring data-processing control type.

The first harsh judgment, then, of computer people is their adulation of computer technology to the point of ignoring the real needs for information systems design. Their first major weakness is their lack of knowledge of business systems. If this charge seems unjust, look at the lists of computer and systems seminars and courses. How often does one see management information included?

The second judgment may even be harsher. It is that despite all the jargon, a great number of computer people know little about the use of computer systems. Here is a check list of possible questions for the computer man.

1 What was the origin of data-based control systems?
2 Has mankind tried other kinds of control systems to control reality?
3 How did the file evolve from earliest times?
4 What part could the files play in an information model of a company?
5 Is a model used for periodic probing or for daily data-processing?
6 How much information in a company is adaptive or periodic and how much is control and continuous?
7 Name several kinds of qualitative information used by senior managers that cannot be expressed in data terms.
8 Name at least three of the major pieces of information a general manager needs every day.
9 Apart from budget, expenditure sales and profit, name three weekly reports that would reach your general manager from your computer. Give the number of pages in each report and the headings.

What this list probes for is an understanding of the place of computers in mankind's control systems. The computer was not just invented: it evolved out of technical progress and invention in response to our information handling needs at a point when the vast size of data models threatened to strangle progress.

In its short history the computer has gone from propellor to jet-age and on into its own space age. In that time two processes have been clearly discernable: the first was that computers were getting smaller and more manageable in size and more powerful in storage and processing capacity; the second was that the job of operating and managing them was growing in complexity in direct proportion to their growth in power and sophistication.

Some years ago the trumpets sounded for yet another generation of computers. These were to make the older generation look like steamrollers. It has since been found that, ingenious as the latest generation computers are, they require a vast amount of supervision by specialist staff, particularly in the area of new software releases from manufacturers.

4 *pressures from within and without*

If we feel that some of the situations described to date have been exceptions rather than the rule, we will be reassured by knowing that the particular process that we will now study will be related to the most successful computer project. From this we must not conclude that most projects reach a stage of technical success—that is, the stage where they are operating in a technically sound manner on schedule. Note that we have said *technically* sound, not *economically* sound. So before we look at such a technically sound operating project and see what happens to it under pressure from itself and its environment, let us briefly mention the many projects that do not reach this stage.

Computer project management is probably improving as more and more books and seminars propose methods for new project managers. What are overlooked most in projects are:

1. Systems planning techniques.
2. The need to use a relevant system for the assessment and control of programming.
3. The need to construct a meaningful operating scheme for live running of jobs after they are programmed.

Stated in its simplest terms: highly sophisticated computers are available ready to plug in. An infinite variety of programs can be written in a great number of forms. Each of these computers comes out of its box to become the central processing stage of a complex operation known as a data processing centre. To ignore the need to design this centre using management science and production control techniques is a common error. Two other common errors are: the neglect of systems planning and programming control. Very little can be said about either of these in this book because of space, but the writer's plea is that he has dealt with them at length elsewhere (*Installing and managing a computer*, Brandon Press, Business Books; *The art of systems analysis*, Prentice-Hall, Business Books).

We will now assume that we are talking about one of the few computer projects that come through on time, as a complete success from the points of view of project control and technical performance. And we are still not looking at ultimate economic feasibility.

The first pressures arise out of the difficult and painful process of taking jobs from the tested or 'pilot run' state into the live or operating state, in other words using real data. During this time, it is necessary to run in a mode known as *parallel*, which is running the old and new together. Programmers and their managers are under extra pressure to deal with the queries that arise during that stage. The number of these is directly related to the number of records that are implemented at one time. It may be courageous to convert a whole billing job to a computer over one week-end, if one has the key-punching staff available to punch up all the files at one time; but before embarking on such a dangerous demonstration a manager should think of the number of queries caused by 'bugs' and simple misunderstandings that will arise. He may find all development, and even all operations, at a standstill while his staff sorts out the real problems.

Systems work that existed in pure abstraction in casual back-rooms suddenly finds itself working side by side with real, live computer operations. As jobs are put live onto the computer, the systems effort tends to slacken in a strange rule that might be known as 'success in systems design invariably brings about the failure of the systems design activity'. Successful systems work increases the load on the computer, increases the attention that senior staff give to computer operations and decreases their interest in systems analyses. There is a very strong case for keeping the systems design team away altogether from the data processing operation, as we will see later.

Internal pressures begin. These can be generated out of several conditions, but the ingredients are there from the beginning in the way the computer staff is made up. No company nowadays will plunge into a computer project without some outside experienced help. Straightaway this introduces the 'insider' and 'outsider' class distinction. Some of the insiders selected by aptitude tests and given the chance of a lifetime at a new career will get cold feet at the last moment and make the emotional decision that they are not going to be able to compete with either the outsiders or their fellow insiders.

This is what the psychologists might call a subconscious decision, for they will produce many reasons for not making a success of the job. The chief one is the charge that only the outsiders are respected, a charge that is dropped a year later when junior insiders start to pass them out and even to leave the company for senior jobs elsewhere. So far, though, we have here no more than the common phenomenon of the reluctant volunteer, the man who has been wanting his break for years and, sadly, perhaps through the way he has been treated in past jobs, cannot take it when it comes along.

A much greater cause of internal stress is the non-technical insider who is transferred to the computer group at a management level to head up systems, say, or operations. If there is also a non-technical computer manager, as there very often is, a perverse, never spoken of 'technical' versus 'management' division emerges. 'You are the technical people', the manager says, 'but we are the administrators and managers'. This sort of distinction makes the technical staff hope that the computer system will collapse so that they can gloat over the panic it would cause in the hearts of their non-technical managers. Another dangerous aspect of this division is the desire of the non-technical manager to keep down the technical people, and his tendency to favour those supervisors who communicate with him in non-technical terms and who are not above criticising the technical people. Here is the worst kind of intrigue, right within the computer department, at its very worst where the top man fears and distrusts his own technicians, and begins to discourage them from doing systems work that will expose them to senior management.

The first major test for the computer department, however, comes from outside, as the user departments begin to complain about the service. There are at least three possible ways in which this takes place:

1 Under a weak computer manager, the computer staff bow their heads, accept the criticism, which is usually pretty strong, examine every charge, and quickly run into the dangerous situation where, through sheer stress, the job can go wrong.

2 Under a strong computer manager, the complaints both true and false, are tossed back with a confidence bordering on contempt, accompanied by proof that the complaining department's input is the worst in the world. This, which is certainly to be recommended if the reader is a computer department manager, but not if he is a user, is known as steamrolling.

3 Under a confused manager, and especially where the user department management is also confused, irrelevant and muddled meetings take place in which general claims are made and general answers given and nothing ever happens.

Anyone who has ever been a computer systems analyst under the last condition truly sees the meaning of bad management, or, more correctly in this case, non-management. Meetings are held, long discussions take place, files of letters written. All letters and minutes reach the programmers eventually, who, if they feel non-management to be the order, simply throw them in the waste basket. Meanwhile, the computer system continues to run calmly, ignoring all the management confusion.

This writer saw one case where the programmers deliberately suppressed all the changes requested and ignored all the criticisms. After six months, a pile of correspondence and many meetings, they had to take the consequences at a top-level investigation. The user manager read a list of the charges: refusing to make ten changes, failure to fix twenty bugs, refusal to answer twenty-five letters. The chief programmer's reply: distrust of the user's ability to understand the system, decision to play it safe and postpone the requested changes for the time being.

And then the final blow as he announced that in support of the programmers' conclusions the computer had been running every day for the six months, pouring out the bills and the customer and salesman reports, and that there were no unusual complaints from the twenty thousand customers in the field, despite the charges of user management.

It takes a tough, confident and rather ruthless computer man to act like the one above, and to be ready at any moment to use the computer's good behaviour as instant proof of the irrelevance of certain management actions; however, such people are not too plentiful, so all too often criticism from the outside mounts to the point where it becomes dangerous to the security of the computer operation.

Irritating but less dangerous pressure comes from the department manager who fears the computer and would welcome its failure. On this note it might be in order to remember that the computer's strongest adversaries will be found not in the union or staff, but amongst department managers. The computer's chief critic, unless he has been appointed data processing manager, may be the accountant. Other managers may also be antagonistic, but generally, unless it is an extraordinary company, managers will be intelligent enough to either take no sides or to offer assistance. The moment cracks begin to show, however, even the friends of the computer pick up stones.

Having established that there is an environment of hostility surrounding even the most efficient system, there is the question of whether the user criticisms are really justified. Like the good manager who compounds the computer myth by joining it without question, the bad user adds to the idea of the computer's omnipotence by his sweeping and exaggerated charges.

The truth is that job performance on the new, expensive computer is very often less than it was when operating under the manual scheme. A major reason for this is the thorny problem of *turnaround times*. Another big factor is the lack of file accessibility. If the job has been taken from a user department and now operates in a new computer building, the time it takes the input and output to travel between the two buildings must be added to the turnaround time. It may be found that the time gained by using a computer is lost by this extra data travel time. We are speaking only about those systems that cannot justify the use of on-line data transmission facilities, which amounts to most systems.

Even systems that use data transmission facilities suffer from the second problem of lack of file accessibility. Under the old scheme the user could look at his records any time he wished. In stores, say, he could look at the ledger records. Now he has to ask the computer department to print out the contents of certain file records from where they are sitting, inaccessible without the computer, on disks or tapes. Even if data transmission lines are employed, he cannot get access to the record at will, unless the computer department keeps the file on-line at all times, which is a very expensive data retrieval solution, only employed for certain specialised jobs where a whole computer system is dedicated to one application, such as airline reservations.

As user complaints about poor performance mount, new and subtle pressure comes from another source. The computer manufacturer's salesman begins to suggest that more hardware would solve turnaround and accessibility problems.

Now comes the real test for the computer manager, for the pressure from the friendly salesman is the memory of an earlier, probably forgotten invitation: stay on the side of your computer man, trust him and go forward with him, and he will support you against your adversaries and help you gain promotion.

And the computer manager can be forgiven if also in the invitation he imagines a threat: refuse to go forward with us and——.

If the computer manager's earlier recommendation to top-management for the order of the particular hardware was in any way inadequate, or based on the wrong reasons, he may now find himself in a position where there is no turning back from a course of expansion.

5 *the great technological breakthrough*

When operating is well under way the computer manager is truly committed to a new world where reality begins to replace mythology. 'I know', the stores manager will say, 'it's a very good system with great potential, but the facts are that I'm getting my figures two hours later than in the past and I can't look at my records any more. On top of this I've saved no staff.'

At this stage the computer manager does not even bother to use the mirages of future stock forecasting and the need to include the stores job in the beautiful total abstraction of production control, because he knows that the stores manager is aware that he is stretched to the limit just keeping what he has on the computer.

This is a central and vital problem, known as program maintenance, which arises out of changes to the programs. Earlier changes can be caused by a variety of reasons, but later changes are caused by the demands of the environment, channelled chiefly through the user.

We must look back to a strange law that we invented earlier about successful systems work causing failure to systems work, and use a variation of it to explain the perversities of the program change process. The greater the systems and programming progress at an early stage in a project, the less it will be at later stages, simply because every program written raises the amount of maintenance and 'one-off' work to be done.

Some people find it very difficult to accept the need for program changes, especially highly qualified members of computer societies. A good computer society man will say that programming changes point to inadequacies in the system; so, incidentally, do new computer operating managers. The computer society man actually believes that the programs, the system and the world can be made to conform to a set of known laws with no unknown variables, no changes to conditions and no new rules.

So strong is this belief, so often does confusion reign in this matter of program changes, and so vital is the point to our whole discussion on the economies of computer systems, that further examination of the causes of these changes is necessary. To recap, the two kinds of demands are: changes to the program demanded by the user, and periodic one-off special jobs. Let us see what these tell us about the world in which computers operate.

How are the changes to the programs caused? Leaving out programming errors or 'bugs', which sooner or later diminish to the point where they are not of great concern, we have the following reasons.

1 The new system is either completely new or it is the old system with some changes. In either case the user will now begin to see that what he is getting is not quite what he wanted in the first place.
2 The old system was accepted because it was there. Suddenly the user sees that it is possible to adapt and change his system through requests to the programmer.
3 The user plays with the system.
4 The user uses the system, the programmer, the programs and the computer as an expensive way of 'de-bugging' his mind, or working out what he really wants.

Any one of these could cause program changes to continue to the point where up to one quarter of the programming staff is kept busy on maintenance and one tenth on special one-off reports.

If one considers the one-off report itself and asks what it is, it can be appreciated that the probe-type management response is the adaptive process through which management tries to adjust the enterprise to the changing environment. The number of special probes or studies, or merely questions from above, that are of a non-recurring, and therefore bad for data-processing nature, is far higher than most people imagine. It runs at around two hundred a year in companies of up to 100 million dollars turnover. Many of these reach the computer. What was the cost of this kind of occurrence in that situation? How many units of this or that? And so on.

The computer society analyst will reply that all these needs should be anticipated in a data base, which is science fiction dreaming. Only a fortune teller can know what the future researcher will probe for. The reality is high program change and frequent requests for one-off jobs, but let us look at the development—maintenance equation.

Once again our progress-stopping progress law comes into play. Here is how it works:

If 24 programmers work hard and bring 400 programs into being, they automatically create maintenance work for six programmers and create the conditions that give rise to one-off requests that will occupy two programmers. If half of them leave over a two-year period for other jobs, which is by no means unusual, the situation will be: 12 experienced programmers, zero to 12 trainees: therefore two-thirds of the experienced staff on maintenance and one-off jobs.

As we will see later this situation is compounded by other factors such as market state, and so on. Meanwhile, it is almost a question of running hard to stay in the same place.

During this second phase where reality begins to replace the myth or the ideal, the morale curve of the computer staff responds with the certainty of a mathematical law. In the beginning, with few exceptions morale soared. The exceptions as we noted earlier were in the inevitable few dissenters who decided that they were not going to make it. Although, as we saw, they will have various explanations for this, the most common will be the complaint that the outsiders are disloyal to the company and loyal only to the computer industry.

As the projects get under way, and particularly as the trainee programmers experience the first triumph of seeing their programs work, morale climbs to a high point, shortly after the installation of the computer and the implementation of their first programs. It then begins to fall.

There are several reasons for this. One is common to all technical projects from computers to space programs. The promise of great future technological glories is past. The computer is in, the moon is conquered and unless Mars is scheduled the programmers want to leave. All kinds of excuses are found. The management is stupid, sometimes known to be true, the pay rates are below the market figure, which is always based on the last highest paying advertisement seen, and there is no obvious line of promotion to top management.

The computer industry, though, suffers above all from the effects of change, that force which continuously undermines stability. The advertisements, the success stories, the free car at another company and higher pay.

The results are dissatisfaction, gloom, rumours, discussions in the corridors, reduced output, all helped by the recent strain of overwork during the implementation stage. The computer manager begins to believe his friendly salesman. The only cure for morale is the cure that he also needs for computer performance: what is known as the *great technological breakthrough*.

Before we look at this course of action we must look again at the position of systems performance during this phase of reality. Not only is job performance reduced through slower turnaround and inaccessibility, but often it is found that computer performance and capacity are below earlier expectations. It must be stressed that the reasons for this are mainly in the application of the computer to the jobs, its *effective* use, rather than any intrinsic failure in the computer's *potential*.

First, it will be found that earlier estimates of speed and

capacity were over-optimistic. Jobs will be taking longer than expected, and taking up more space in main processing memory and on-line storage. If it is a multi-programming environment, in which two or more jobs are run together, main memory may be quickly exhausted by the extra software needs, and effective turnaround times inadequate.

One common example of the latter is seen in early ideal theories of optimum queuing, where all jobs are first fed in, processed in an optimum manner, and only then printed out. Far short of this ideal is the reality of the working environment, where clerks, needed to check edit listings and final outputs, simply cannot wait for the computer to choose *its* optimum output times. The people, and the world, work a nine-to-five day, so who do we blame if that is not an optimum state for a computer that has a 24-hour daily cycle?

When the first serious results of the reality stage begin to show, which are that all the jobs announced to go on the computer will not fit onto it, the computer manager, if he was involved in the original hardware specification or selection, may feel tempted to move on. The computer industry is full of jokes about the man who has five jobs in six years. Anyone can install a computer, but the real challenge is to ensure that the computer fits the demands of the job it was intended to do.

If he cannot move on, or has no desire to, he must face up to the fact that all the promised goods will not be delivered by means of the particular hardware on hand, and may employ the great technological breakthrough solution.

This is, of course, to project new targets for new systems, increased savings and efficiency, and to apply to top management for permission to buy more hardware. Management's reaction may vary, depending on whether they have gone through the two stages covered later, called 'the management response' and 'the post-mortem'. We will assume for the moment that they accept, pushed delicately by the computer manager, perhaps, by his suggestion that if a course of continued expansion is not embarked upon, the staff may all leave. It will be decided, of course, to announce the expansion, not in terms of poor initial plans, inadequate capacity, and earlier false optimism, but as a further wise technological step.

If the computer manager, or project leader, has narrowly avoided trouble up to now, he may be really heading for it this time. The expansion may take many forms. Here are some:

1 A second, smaller computer to take up the work still to be done.
2 More main storage, called memory, and extra on-line storage units, in the hope of multi-programming.
3 Multi-programming facilities and data-transmission.
4 A larger computer.
5 Another computer of the same size and capacity.

The first is usually disastrous, for there will be no compatibility between hardware, software, or files. The second is a possibility, although fraught with dangers, particularly that all the new sophisticated software needed to run such an advanced system may itself exhaust the extra capacity purchased. This means that more main storage is bought to house more complex equipment and to do more work, but the special software programs needed to make it work and to run more than one job, take up so much of the newly acquired main memory space, that there is no room for the extra programs to do the extra work.

The third has exactly the same dangers, plus the added fact that on-line data transmission uses even more software, and demands that files be on-line all the time, creating the need for very large, and very expensive, on-line storage units, such as disks and tapes.

The fourth could be the most disastrous of all. It is most expensive, sometimes the most expensive, depending on the size of the models in question. If the jobs are largely input-output bound, that is, their throughput speeds are largely dependent on the time it takes to read in the input and read out the output, it may be found that the increase in speed and capacity is minimal and that one has paid out a lot of money in exchange for idle time or 'wait state' time on a bigger and faster central processor that cannot be properly utilised.

The last, which is exactly double the cost of one computer, as the system is now two, is by far the surest, if one can ignore economics. The shrewd manager who knows this may employ the great technological breakthrough to the fullest by claiming, not that he is short of time and capacity, but that he intends to expand the company's computer operations beyond the company, by selling computer time to others.

It takes nerve and confidence, but properly handled this new myth can take in everybody right up to the general manager, who may be struck by what this move will do for the company's public image. Here, at last, for any one computer manager at least, is where the Cinderella story can actually come true. This piece of strategy can work and pay handsome dividends, for the simple reason that, although using a computer may not be profitable, selling time on it certainly is.

Where a company may be paying only a quarter, or even a tenth, of normal rental for time used after the main nine-to-five shift, it can sell that time for double what it pays for normal shift. This means it can sell time available during normal shift at a good profit, and time on the other two shifts and weekends at a really high profit. If it is selling to customers who do their own programming, it is a very easy way indeed to make money.

The computer manager can exploit the vast market of people who, not able to justify a computer themselves, desire the prestige of associating themselves with one. Government agencies, local government groups, engineers working for urban authorities, state-sponsored research groups, university lecturers, schools, operations research men, market research teams, economists, econometricians, statisticians, and so on, many of them with inefficient simulation models of the economy or the environment that eat up the weekend and late shift at up to three hundred dollars an hour. The computer operation is now profitable, for, no longer just in the computer using business, it is in the highly profitable business of computer selling.

[illegible] for the time of a [illegible] or a [illegible] [illegible] process that cannot be properly [illegible].

The [illegible], which is exactly double the [illegible] the company [illegible] [illegible] [illegible], as [illegible] [illegible] [illegible] economics. The [illegible] [illegible] the [illegible] [illegible] through [illegible] [illegible] [illegible] [illegible] [illegible] [illegible] [illegible] [illegible] [illegible] [illegible] to expand the [illegible] [illegible] [illegible] company [illegible] [illegible] [illegible].

It takes [illegible] and [illegible] [illegible] [illegible] can [illegible] everybody [illegible] up to the [illegible] [illegible] who [illegible] [illegible] by what the [illegible] will do [illegible] [illegible] [illegible] [illegible] [illegible] [illegible] [illegible] [illegible] [illegible] [illegible] [illegible] [illegible] [illegible] story [illegible] [illegible] [illegible] [illegible] [illegible] [illegible] [illegible] [illegible] [illegible]

When a company [illegible] [illegible] [illegible] [illegible] [illegible] [illegible] [illegible] and [illegible] [illegible] [illegible] [illegible] [illegible] [illegible] [illegible] [illegible] [illegible] for [illegible] [illegible] at [illegible]

[illegible] statisticians [illegible] in the [illegible] [illegible] the business of company [illegible].

6 *the management response*

Only a few companies, unfortunately, have managers with the kind of vision that steers a computer project out of its age of reality difficulties onto a course that puts the company right into the computer business. The vast majority drift on into the management response stage. If any good computer project manager operating under a wise top management is still reading at this stage, he might keep his patience by being reminded that we are still discussing the failures, and that we will be praising him in due course.

The management response stage is reached in those companies where top management has paid little or no attention to the computer project since the board signed the order for the system. One of their few contacts with the computer department may have been at the official opening ceremonies, where, accompanied by the directors, they inspected the computer, and after suitable speeches and press releases, declared the computer to be on the air, while the programmers muttered typical responses in the background.

After that date they may have sat back, ignored the need to name a good senior official to report to the general manager as responsible for computer operations, and issued no policy directives for new systems.

The computer staff will have been hired *after* the signing of the order for the system and *after* the designation of the original projects. In time, only the computer staff know how the computer should be used to best suit the demands of the company. Unless they have the support of top management and the power of policy directives, doors will be shut against them, as managers will be either too busy, too disinterested or too hostile to allow appraisals and investigations of their departments to take place.

The systems planning process demands that both long- and short-term plans be projected by the systems planning staff. These plans have two very important uses: firstly, they are the basis for work schedules, and, secondly, the systems they contain reflect the structure of whatever data base and information system are being constructed. Without a plan, jobs may even be programmed in the wrong order, so that certain jobs cannot be implemented because they depend on other jobs being put into operation first.

So, in the drifting enterprise, the systems planners project plans and, passing them up the line, wait expectantly for acceptance, modification or rejection. In far too many cases they are met with silence or indifference. The plan may have got to the top and been pushed aside by a busy general manager or president. It may have been ignored by a vice-president who at that stage was not interested in the computer as part of his political career. It may not even have got past the computer manager because he was unable to respond to anything other than whatever was necessary to his daily existence.

Without formal acceptance from the top the analysts cannot even carry out initial appraisals in the departments in which proposed systems are housed. Without policy directives, doors will stay closed. Analysts begin to grumble, asking why this particular company bought a computer in the first place, and why they are employed.

If this state continues for a couple of years after implementation, until the eventual management response, computer staff attitudes will pass from the 'What are we here for?' stage to the one where they decide to stop banging their heads against a brick wall. We will see what effects this has, if we break up the computer specialists into approximately three groups—the excellent, the good and the middling-to-bad.

During the initial phase the excellent, who may number no more than one or two in fifty, are fired with confidence and enthusiasm. They emanate this, affecting those around them, and they sweep away opposition, arousing admiration, envy and much hostility. They impress their own superior, or superiors, often to the point where it is secretly decided that they are dangerous competition and must go.

The good, caught up with the mood, grow in stature and ability, proving that most intelligent and balanced people expand if given a chance, and that job enrichment is the highest motivation. With a few exceptions, the middling-to-bad improve, especially when the good ones begin to move out to other jobs, so that it becomes obvious, in the face of so many vacant seats, that even they can be promoted.

To really measure the extent of how much a company loses through mis-handling its computer system, we must look hard at what the excellent people could mean to them. Here, for the first time perhaps in the history of a company, are one or two highly motivated trained senior systems designers or managers, who, during the project, are beginning to understand how the company's information and control systems worked and how it could be improved.

Here are a couple of excellent people whose ideas alone could now be worth more than the cost of the hardware they control, or could help to control given the right incentives, designing systems plans that are being ignored, passing from a state of enthusiasm to frustration as weeks pass with no intelligent response from above.

A sad, though extreme consequence, is disappointment, gloom, worry, frustration, leading to ulcers or worse. It is respectfully suggested, however, that no senior systems designer is morally obliged to get into such a state over the lack of response from management.

The other outcome could be that he decides to stop trying to sell his and his staff's services to an employer who does not want them, and to take the only course of action that seems proper and moral in the circumstances. This is to start his own company.

These are the men that have founded the thriving new software, programming service, and education industries. They have opened up new university departments, started publishing houses, and even, eventually, purchased banks. Of course they are not bitter about their former employers. 'Indeed', they will remark, 'we must be grateful to our old company, for had they been interested in their computer, we would have all gone on pouring our efforts into it. Now look at what we have achieved.'

Amongst these and amongst the good systems analysts under them are some of the best minds to be found in industry today. They can take a problem, examine it, air possible solutions, discard them unemotionally as they find each flaw, and search, patiently, for the one that is optimum or nearest the optimum. They can be clear and concise: they can separate the wheat from the chaff, and, inhuman though it might seem, talk with relentless logic and commonsense in a world that lives on its nerves at times. The source of their certainty—the computer system.

Even when they work in a good environment under a knowledgeable management, there is no room for them to move upward, as it is unusual for senior systems analysts or managers to be promoted up into top management. Indeed, even if top management had such a wish, there could hardly be room for the promotion of such a large concentrated pool of technical expertise as one finds in the computer department. Many fairly low-ranking programmers earn more money than line managers with higher status on the organisation chart.

Faced with this wide-based, low apex, pyramid, good middle and junior staff tend to seek promotion by moving to higher paid jobs elsewhere, and good senior men face up to the inevitable move sideways—often out into partnerships or on their own.

Before the management response takes place, the conditions for failure are very often already assured. The hardware is in, the system is working, but how secure is the staff? And how many companies appreciate the value of such a trained staff on their own premises, and the vacuum that will be left in its absence? By the time such facts are realised, the project can be a loss-making maintenance operation with no hope of any foreseeable development schemes. The full reasons for this will be seen later when we look at the total programmer market picture.

When, at last, criticism from user departments, general rumours, and the obvious facts that neither savings nor targets have been achieved, are forced upon the consciousness of top management, the long awaited response takes place. And here we might look at the familiar control loop.

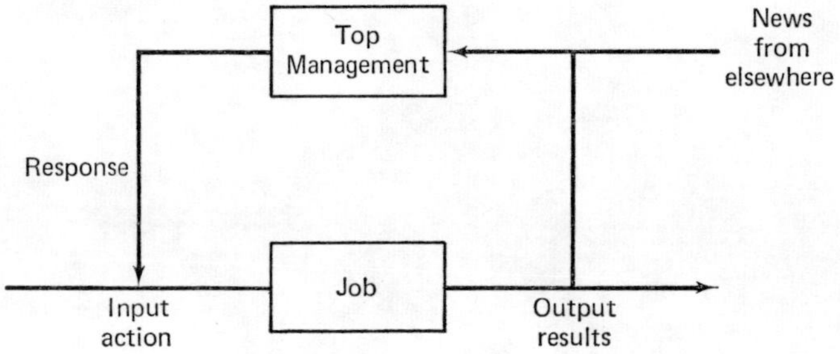

If there is no response, the job may just drift on, maintained by its operators. If due response is poor the job or system may oscillate, but if due response is so late that the horse has left the stable, it is a worthless gesture.

The last can be seen when top management, having either ignored systems plans, or demanded none for several years, suddenly asks for everything including the mythical MIS system, after all the good people have left and the computer department staff is hard-put just trying to keep operations going. The computer staff, of course, at this stage, laugh heartily at the final acceptance of their existence. When the true condition of the computer project becomes apparent, the time has come for 'The post-mortem'.

7 *the post–mortem*

A little known law of life is that of irreversibility. No human or physical act or process can be reversed so that objects and states end up as they were. During the original act and in the time just after it, both object and state undergo change that is irreversible. An early and widely known poem, *Humpty-dumpty*, recognises this. Once the egg is broken, that is that.

It is the same with systems. They can never be reversed. They can be changed, certainly, and sidetracked, and they can be very easily destroyed. The moment a human-machine information system comes into being, it takes on a life of its own independent of its creators. The operators just run it, while programmers merely maintain it. The process called *entropy* begins, a confusion that can be measured by the growing gulf between what people first knew about the system and now know about it.

During the system specification and programming phase, the analysts got to know more about the job than anyone before or after. After the job went on the air, knowledge of the job began to decline for several normal reasons, plus one dangerous new reason. The normal reasons were the analysts and programmers turning to new jobs, and forgetting this one. There is no way to avoid this. A rule could be made that a programmer must stay with a job for ever. Even if he did not quit immediately, he would soon not know as much about it as he used to, simply because later on it requires only maintenance work.

The dangerous new reason is that even the user's job knowledge now starts on its decline. He used to have the job in his own department, with all the processes or job steps known to his clerks, and all the records and files on open cards or in easily accessible ledgers all around. Take such simple information as job attributes—height, colour, average price, average movement, and so on, and summary information—number of this, amount of that, by this or that category or state.

All of this now is hidden on tapes or disks. If he used to extract it every quarter or half year or periodically in the past, he might soon forget that it is available. He might even begin to forget what the job attributes and information summaries are. His information has been taken over by data processors, who may no longer have any interest in it, for the truth may be that their interest in giving him valuable new information was the excuse for their expensive new computer.

So in a short time the change agents, the computer staff, have become reactionaries. During their selling phase they were quick to charge reluctant users with an unwillingness to accept change. Now, burdened with the new system, realising that no savings can be made by just maintaining what is on the computer, and perhaps understaffed, they discourage changes sometimes to the point of refusing to accept any at all.

Even if they are not understaffed, they become aware of the creeping entropy that threatens their system, the growing confusion. And so aware of their diminishing knowledge of what is in the system, they are afraid to change it, and would simply rather leave it alone. If the reader feels that this is exaggerated, he can be assured that this is now the programming manager part of the writer speaking, who knows that other programming managers will have also felt a cold breeze at the thought of changing some running programs. He knows that the myth of the world run by computers automatically is a piece of science fiction, for he is aware that all systems have one natural tendency—towards disintegration.

At this stage, the technical staff welcomes confused management, meetings between the managers of the men that know what is going on in the user department and the managers of those that know what is going on, and definitely not going on, in the computer department. The message is so confused by the time it reaches the systems analysts that they have a good excuse for ignoring it. All of which makes the frustration of the user who wants some change or improvement, a new set of reports perhaps, or a better turnaround, more acute.

Finally top management finds that criticism has reached the stage mentioned in the last chapter where it must deal with the computer. They talk to the computer department manager, learn some of the truth about how the computer project really stands. He, of course, if he has not been warning them often, must either look for a new job, or begin a program of contrived confusion. Suspecting the last, perhaps, top management call in outside consultants to perform a costly investigation of the computer project. This is known as 'the project audit and evaluation stage'. In fact it is often a head-hunting operation.

They may decide not to use outside consultants, but instead to depend upon their own staff. They may choose the chief accountant, for example, to report on the financial results of the project, or they may even call upon the internal audit staff. The last may compound the confusion even further.

From the time the project started the auditors will have been around, in many cases genuinely interested in the welfare of the company's control system, but, unfortunately, in many other cases also interested in getting themselves a computer education. They are hardly to be blamed for the last, seeing the number of auditing companies now offering larger salaries for the auditor computer consultant. Regardless of what good he may do himself, however, and may do future employers, the contribution of such an auditor to a computer department can often be measured in totally negative terms.

For one thing, he can gain little more than a general knowledge of either the expertise needed to plan and manage a computer or of that needed to design systems and programming.

He will thus pick up the kind of knowledge that will send him into endless loops of debate and confusion and succeed in earning him the dislike and irritation of the computer staff.

The auditor's most annoying device, by far, is his questionnaire. Obtained from accountants' institutes and certain textbooks, this ranges over hundreds of questions on organisation and control. Some of the questions, however, are designed to infuriate the most patient systems manager. Some examples are:

> Do you get a weekly report of maintenance from the computer engineer?
>
> What proof have you got that he has maintained the computer properly?

The answer to the first is no, the answer to the second, none whatsoever. The two questions, however, and those that follow illustrate that the auditor is trying to apply his old experiences to a new world.

> Do you allow programmers access to the computer room?
>
> Do you allow programmers access to the computer console?

The answer to the first is that people are restricted from entering the computer room, but for reasons of dust and distraction, not the ones the auditor has in mind. The answer to the second is that only a really unthinking computer manager would allow anybody to press a button on the console with a full job stream going.

The auditor who asks these questions pictures an old-fashioned criminal type of programmer creeping into the computer room and distorting the data by manipulating programs and files by means of the console typewriter. Any programmer that wanted to distort either data or files could do it with his pencil on his coding sheets, hundreds of miles from the computer. There is very little anyone could do about the matter, except to make sure that the *system* is designed to safeguard against such possibilities.

If the auditor, then, is called upon to investigate the computer project, real issues may become buried under generalisations about 'controls' and 'audit trails' and 'restricted access' and so on.

Top management can, of course, turn to the computer manufacturer for advice during the post-mortem. Indeed the computer manufacturer would be only too pleased to suggest causes and solutions, in a far more detailed manner than an auditor, and based on the best technical reasoning. The only snag is that the solution will invariably be to buy more hardware.

Indeed, this is exactly what may happen in those cases where there is a good understanding and relationship between a key manager and the manufacturer, particularly if the manufacturer is prepared to stand by the manager should the finger be pointed at him during this difficult stage.

With no such relationship between a key manager and the manufacturer, it is even possible that the manufacturer's top man might drop a word in the ear of the company's general manager, to the effect that 'the project now appears to be flagging somewhat, and that perhaps it needs some new stimulus'. It need hardly be said that an indelicate remark at this stage about a computer manager under suspicion from the top could do serious harm. Manufacturers, aware of the implications of such situations, and, of course, aware that things can swing in both directions, exercise extreme tact and care at this stage.

During this stage also a confused management could become the victim of other manufacturers—known as the *competition* to whatever manufacturer is supplying the existing hardware and service. Amongst possible illusory courses of action that might be presented by competitive manufacturers are:

Faster and cheaper hardware.
Better support service.
Faster and more advanced input techniques.

In a time of stress, one simple rule can be applied by management to help decide whether *any* hardware innovation would have a real effect on the economy of the project. It is that if the change needs the time of computer staff, that time should be costed and deducted from a reasonably reduced promised saving. The point here is that *development* costs are very high. New systems seldom last more than a few years; development that is purely changeover should be avoided unless it promises significant savings.

Wise management will not need to turn to auditors and manufacturers, but will be able to trust its own computer staff. The management that let this state develop may not trust its computer staff anymore, so may turn to outside help for the post-mortem. The only outsiders to turn to apart from the manufacturers are the consultants.

There was once a general manager who boasted to a systems analyst that he had foiled all the greedy computer manufacturers by training one of his own staff as a computer expert and having him examine the proposals. The cynical systems analyst spoiled the poor man's lunch by pointing out the things mentioned in the first chapter of this book, not the least of which was the expert's intention of staying firmly in the computer industry. The general manager, intelligent enough to immediately grasp this fact, was upset and asked, 'Who do you trust then?' and the systems analyst replied, 'Outside consultants, who have no ladder to climb in your company'. The general manager was pleased and bought the systems analyst a drink.

Now that systems analyst wishes to confess that he also had been guilty of some naïvety. Most computer consultants are also motivated by self-interest. Their interest in the audit of a computer project will certainly be the improvement of that project, but it will also be to obtain further assignments in the company, whether it can be improved or not.

Straightaway, we must say that if they do improve the computer project, they should be given further assignments that may improve the company, but we must remember that they may not be able to improve the project, for reasons mentioned earlier and for more to come.

First of all, there is hardly a consultant who will take an initial look at the system and say, 'All is well, or as well as it could be under the circumstances, so that will be five hundred dollars please and now we will leave you to carry on'. There is a good chance that they will find plenty of weaknesses; if they find none, however, they may be tempted to invent some or to use 'sin is bad' and 'virtue good' themes.

Then there is the danger that they may use key people or be used by them. The villain, if any, for example, could tempt them with promises of more assignments for them: the hero, if any, or honest man, may end up writing their reports. If they are employed by a senior manager, they may propose that the computer should be under him, which could make his position difficult regarding proposals for further work. If a manager favours them too much, he could split his own staff and lose the loyalty of his best people.

And finally, they may be the ones who also operate a turnkey and facilities scheme, such as one discussed in the next chapter.

8 *into the arms of the facility merchants*

A facilities operator offers computer users several services. He may do systems design work, programming, or even manage computer operations. It is a good business with a very good potential. Good, that is, depending on whether you are in the facilities business or just trying to run a computer.

If you are in the facilities business, it is best to start with the small computer user. As there is a minimum cost to every computer user in achieving expertise, the smaller user suffers most. He is most likely, at the beginning at least, to turn to outside help, which, as we will see, will be very difficult for him to relinquish.

If the manufacturer, especially the large one, is allowed to go on giving this help, it will be difficult for you to get the business; however, as the manufacturer is already pretty over-stretched, through staff losses, and, more important, as he charges for his help, you should employ two tactics. First, charge less than him, next, steal his staff by offering them higher salaries.

On the other hand, if you are a user, and want to look after yourself, you also should steal from the manufacturer, for the more men you leave him with, the more computers he will sell, so that even more companies will be stealing from you.

Despite all your efforts, though, you may still end up being handled by a facilities group, for reasons which we will now see. It is very difficult to operate a computer independently in the computer industry. All kinds of strange things happen: the hardware may be blamed, the software, the programs, the electric current, dust, humidity, and mice in the air-conditioning system. Imagine a situation where you are having some inexplicable trouble, such as a file refusing to be read, and the engineer and his company suggest that it is neither hardware nor software, but your programs, your dust or your fluctuating electric current.

The process of using computers is like programming, which is a logical way of looking at life. Life, or living, can largely be thought about in programming terms as a series of two-way decisions. Is it this? If not, is it that? The experienced systems manager or data-processing manager, if he is an ex-programmer, quickly finds that, while perhaps not naming an exact source of trouble, he can localise it and can prove, beyond all doubt, what it cannot be. To do this he needs at least two of everything, and the more the better.

If, for example, one of the disk drives was giving trouble, and the engineer said, 'It's your bad electricity', the manager immediately orders the disk pack switched to the other drives. If it never happens on them, it is not the electricity, not can it be the programs, nor the humidity: it must be a bad disk drive.

If, however, it is not happening on any single device, but at random across the devices, or in main memory, he must turn to other computers. For as long as he is alone and independent, he can ring up the managers of other computer systems like his own. If he finds that they also have the trouble, he then knows that it is not his programs.

This is not an easy job, however, and usually only the skilled manager of a large computer department is equipped for such complex diagnoses. The smaller computer user is almost completely in the computer manufacturer's arms. He will not only pay the manufacturer for the hardware he buys, but he will also pay for any systems and programming services they provide, and even for the education they give him. If his system is not profitable, and if he expands it in an attempt to make it profitable, he could end up paying the manufacturer to educate him in those techniques that will cause him to increase the manufacturer's profit and decrease his own. It is only one step away from paying the computer salesman to come and sell him a computer.

The small user who appreciates this vulnerability is an excellent target for the facilities supplier. The facilities supplier begins by writing some or all of his programs for him, but the whole process must be looked at from the beginning.

The small user is often the most enthusiastic and *naïve* of all. Even incompetent and confused managers in large companies have had enough experience to know that reality always falls far short of promised ideals. The small user may appoint one of his staff, an accountant perhaps, as part-time computer specialist, and then hire his hardware.

Much as the manufacturer would like to do all his systems and programming for him, thereby assuring a lifelong wedlock, he cannot, as he must deploy his overstretched forces in their prime function of hardware selling. As he will invariably sell the most sophisticated machine as the customer's job, budget and the competition allows, he will give rise to a systems and programming load that neither he nor the customer can handle with existing staff.

The facilities supplier can now step in and offer his services. Once he begins, his chances of getting all of the systems and programming work are very good, for the simple reason that the customer liaison man cannot set up a complimentary programming force. Administrative and general systems details will mount to the point where the customer's man becomes a mere representative, dealing with user manager requirements, reporting back to the facilities suppliers. In many cases they may move right into the company with him for the initial systems work.

All this time the customer manager is under the illusion that his man, who is to be his computer specialist, is 'learning about programming' and 'learning about the new computer systems' so that he can 'train others within the company'. And also during this time, the customer liaison man is working hard on his computer history *resumé* as he now fully realises that this is his chance for a career in the computer world.

The truth dawns abruptly when he gives notice. The user management realises that, not only has it no systems and programming expertise, but that it lacks even operating expertise. The facility suppliers thereupon offer an operating service also. What the user may not yet have realised, however, is that his chances of ever getting control of his own systems and programs now are very slim. First, the only way one can really cope with the maintenance demands of computer programs is by training programmers to write new programs, and, second, the market may not allow him to ever build up an effective development and support team as we will see later on.

Even with the larger user there is room for the facility supplier as targets are not met and programmer turnover climbs. It is quite possible, however, that the consultants that may be called in to carry out the post-mortem may be the ones to set off the facility operation.

The range of facilities as we noticed is very great, the profitability of each depending on several factors and always on the availability of trained personnel on the market. The best business by far is that of offering systems support only—there is no programming, so you cannot be caught in the programmer-shortage vicious circle; there is no computer to be operated, and therefore no hardware or production problems.

The programming business is highly profitable, but full of the dangers that the user is exposed to. One can quickly get bogged down with good current, and profitable, business, but be unable to expand. Program development is good and bad in as much as it can give rise to program maintenance and support.

If the user is not to be shocked at the size of the program maintenance quotation, then the facilities supplier has underquoted. It is a good business for the supplier if he has quoted well, for it can be lifelong; it is bad because it further ties down his scarce staff.

Less desirable for just ease of operation, but also quite profitable, is the operating facility. This could even lead to the ultimate possibility that the hardware itself be removed from the customer's premises and that all operations be carried out by the facilities supplier, perhaps over transmission lines on a 'time-sharing' basis.

Now let us have a look at the far-reaching effects of some or all of these moves on the company's information system. We will begin with the original user and end up with the ultimate operation. This is the position just before conversion to one's own computer.

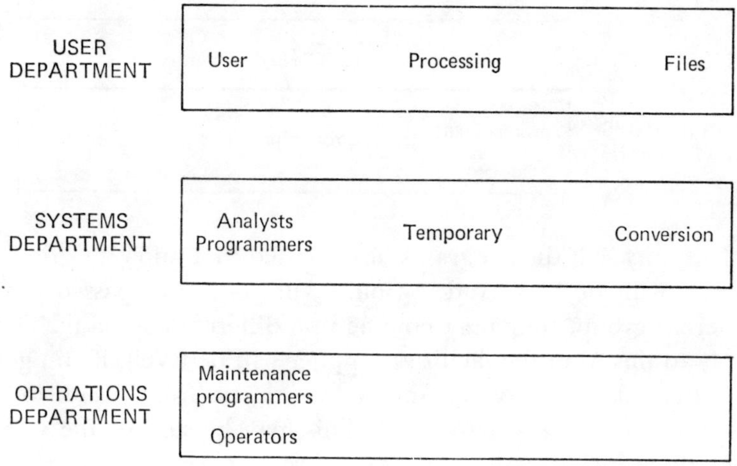

Already a tremendous change is taking place. All of the processing and all of the files are moving to the operations department. Here they no longer get the full attention of their original custodians, and get less and less attention from the analyst who converted them as time passed. In the operating department each is only one of many other jobs.

Now let us look back at the last picture and consider the position after a facilities supplier does the systems and programming work. It will be slightly worse, if he leaves after programming, insofar as we may know even less about what is in our programs and files. But now consider, if he not only programs the jobs, but runs them on our, or his, computer.

Here is the position before he takes over.

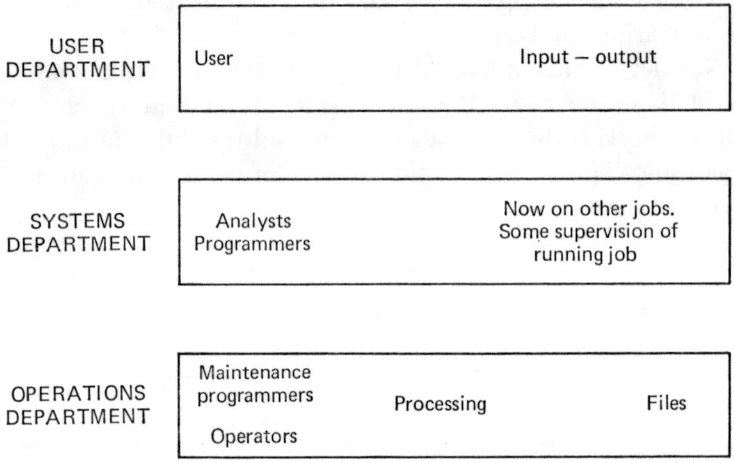

Not only will the programs have passed to a different group, so also will the files. And not only will both have passed to a different group, they may now be in a different company. The reply to this from the facilities supplier will be 'Well, if you get a better job done by us, and more interest from us in your information systems, why not?' This may be so, but the very thought of it is enough to take one's breath away. And perhaps, as we will see later, it is the direction in which we have to go after all.

Our consultant may or may not offer us a facilities service in addition to his post-mortem advice. Whether he does or not, he has definitely got the best arrangement, so far, even after the manufacturer, who while being far richer, is also far more hardworked.

The easiest job is to give advice even when we are right. And to support this the writer must add that he had sat up all night programming, and stood up all night debugging compilers, and lived the frustrating life of a systems manager, and that to write this book is far easier and more pleasant than any of those jobs.

Any consultant can come along and advise on how it should not have been done. There is only one course of action for the computer manager who finds himself the victim of such advice. He should tell his general manager to get the consultant to agree to his fees being charged on a time saved, or programming output increased, or targets met basis.

9 *the computer*

Most computer books for managers go through the old routine of explaining that the computer is made up of an arithmetic unit, a logic unit, and so on. Some computer educators agree that it really leaves the reader, and in many cases the writer, where he started from. After writing two several-volume works explaining computers and systems with other authors, this writer has no intention of trying to put the computer over in popular concepts of logic units and arithmetic units. For one thing, it seems certain that nothing that is really worthwhile can be learned in this way, and, for another and more important reason, its *uses* and *meaning* in the modern world should first be explained and examined before its working needs to be explained, if one feels that one needs to know such a thing.

A good way to understand what a computer is, what it does, and how it works, is to ignore it completely, and to study the origin and meaning of information systems instead. Indeed, if the computer were more often seen as merely the hardware that housed the information system and gave it its power and speed, much of the confusion and misuse of computer systems might be avoided.

A good point to begin is with man's early cave pictures. No one really knows why they were drawn, but a very interesting guess is that they were magic models of a hoped for reality in the world outside. This view attempts to explain why the artist or priest stabbed the animal after the picture was drawn, by drawing in stab wounds and weapons.

If this was the case, the cave picture can be regarded as an attempt to construct the first *control model* of reality for the purpose of controlling it. The control model was manipulated in the cave in the hope or expectation that a caribou would fall under a spear on the plains outside.

There have been many attempts to construct models of reality since then, down the ages, but with few exceptions these were representative models rather than control models. There were mathematical and philosophical models, the latter constructed to justify rather than to explain, and one of these at least helped to sustain a philosophy of permanence that defied change for over a thousand years.

A few models, if they can be called that, did try to control as much as represent. The most striking of these was the dance; however, easy it may be to compare the cave drawing with modern real-time systems where central initiation results in terminal action, dancing for rain or crops seems quite far removed from the simulation and control models of today.

The earliest signs of the kind of information systems we now know were in Mesopotamia where clay tablets show the existence of records that formed groups that represented separate resources or *elements*, like taxes, stocks and the likes. Here already was the concept of a file as well as that of *data*. It seems that one of the great changes brought about by mankind's move from a hunting to settled urban life was the possibility of accumulating heavy containers that could not be carried formerly.

The earliest known such containers, apart from bags and satchels, were, of course, the pots, the results of the art or science known as pottery. These were, perhaps, the first real resource containers of settled urban communities, leading to boxes, bins, and pens, the forerunners of the granneries, oil tanks and other huge resource containers upon which the modern world is based.

The containers are the much overlooked artifacts of the world, just as files are the much overlooked elements of the computer. The file is the record of what is in a resource container, or a resource element, like capital, or creditors. It is inconceivable that a business system, or indeed any economical system, could exist without resources and files that measure and control the resource.

A children's lemonade or soda stand business has liquid and, possibly if they do any business, cash, as its resources.

Resources must first be built up for settled economic business systems to begin. It is said that this most significant historical process, involving the saving of a surplus for re-investment into crops and labour, marked the beginning of the urban revolution that was eventually to change the world from a nomadic to a settled way of life.

If the resource is to be maintained, it must be supported by work or business *events*.

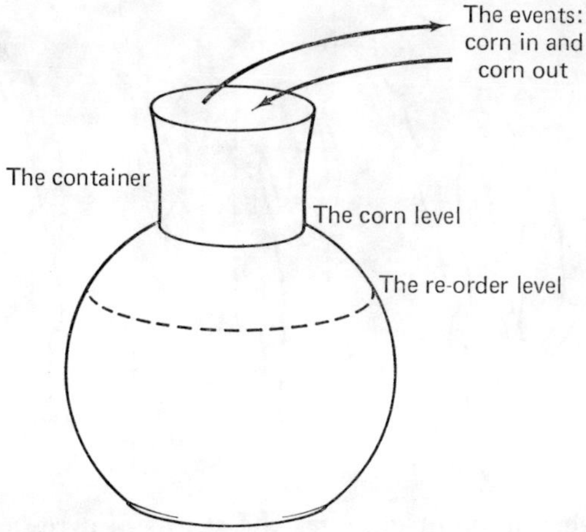

Every manager knows what an event is, although he seldom thinks about it. Every accountant and computer man certainly knows. It is what is often called a *transaction*. The event involves units of time, material and money. The *data* that records the *event*, registers the *number of units in the event* and describes the type of event—that is, what it is for and whether it is out or in, debit or credit.

The unit of measure within the event is the lowest convenient meaningful measure of action, time or substance, such as one bag of coal, rather than one lump or sixty-three lumps, or one pound of butter rather than one ounce.

Whenever an event changes the status of a resource, the file must be adjusted by the data that reflects that event. Camels into and out of the Mesopotamian palace pens meant additions to the camel file and, perhaps, a new camel total.

Some of the resources were so large in the early urban world that the sizes of palace pens became embarrassing. If we con-

sider those pens and palace to be containers that housed edible stocks, and if we also consider that wages were paid with some resource, like goats say, that were used as a means of exchange, we can see why the information system dates back, at least, seven thousand years.

The information system is made up of sub-systems and some over-all summary systems. The palace stocks could be a sub-system, called a system for short. The system is the *set of technical rules* used to relate the event data to the resource data, and to produce required statistics or control output. Typical of such control output, is the setting off of re-orders upon reaching container re-order levels or the sending out of wages or bills.

The whole system is a *complete abstraction*, based on abstract technical information and updated by the abstraction of data. It is a model of reality, just like the caveman's drawing. The high priest, or scribe, or clerk, sits in front of his model, feeds it with input data, extracts output data, and thereby controls the real life situation that the model represents.

The clay tablets or books and ledgers he uses merely house the model, system, or information system, just as the computer merely houses them today. It is the information system that controls, not *the computer*. The computer is the technology that gives man's long-established control systems *speed, power and automation.*

Now that we have seen the part that files play in control systems, let us see why we have to have them. Even before the invention of systems, and even resource containers, man was probably using data to record certain events. Every time he scratched a notch on a slate or stick to record some count condition—each time a count of caribou went beyond the capacity of his ten fingers, say—he was, in fact, using two abstract artifacts that have revolutionised our world.

The first was, of course, the act of using a data symbol to record a logical event grouping, the second was the act of creating a file so that he could record onto it what his fingers and mind could no longer hold, in short, increasing his memory or storage capacity.

Mathematics gave him a powerful method of manipulating his event or source data as was seen in the wonderful engineering and architectural achievements of Egypt. The way he used this constant method of mathematics became his system, to be known in later times as accounting and statistics and other names, but the file was of enormous importance, just as the resource container it described was also.

What the early manager lacked was speed of computation and speed of accessibility to files. The clay tablet, the quill and parchment, the ledger and the spiked documents were often so cumbersome that they were better dispensed with altogether. The medieval man's predicament is interesting to observe.

The medieval merchant-manufacturer may have used three different data systems. The first was in his head. This would account for jobs like production control, scheduling and so on.

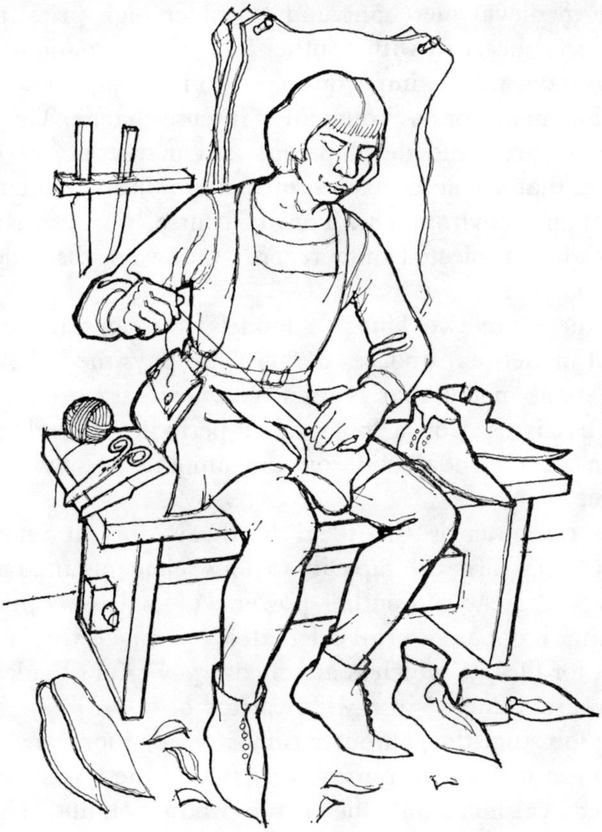

The second used the principle of taking a look. To know the position of his stock of raw materials, say, or finished goods, he would simply look at the shelves or at the floor, and re-order if it seemed that he should.

The third is very interesting, for up to now it has been the only kind known to the clerks and accountants. It was what he owed, what was owing to him, and how much he had in cash. Most likely, he wrote that down.

This accounting information is concerned with past financial performance and current resource status. It is historical and protective, so that clerks and accountants tend to take a passive and reactionary view of business.

The medieval merchant and his older high priest ancestor were also concerned with another kind of information that also needed data, which, important enough in an age of no change, is vital in an age or environment of intense change. This consists of the research and development and marketing, or *adaptive*, analyses that are necessary to constantly adjust an enterprise to its changing environment. This, of course, was also largely in the head or projected onto records that were discarded after each analysis.

So, there are two kinds of models: the constant recurring control model that updates the files and pays the bills, and the 'simulation' model that is used, changed, discarded, and rebuilt, but is used on a 'one-off' or periodic basis, dependent, not on the calendar, but on the amount of environmental change.

The computer is the ideal hardware for an information system: it has large file capacity to house elements and resources, and it has great computing power. A good description of a computer is not a powerful calculator, but an electronic housing system for files, to which is attached a powerful calculator that can be programmed in a wide variety of ways.

The jobs that the computer is most needed for, however, are those most difficult to put onto it: two of the kinds we saw in the medieval merchant's head, the production and scheduling work, and the adaptive planning and research work. The reasons for the first are the immense difficulty in building a model that is truly representative of the production situation, with its near-infinite number of variables, and the cost of gathering the input; the reason for the second is the length of time needed to program a simulation of an environment at any given time. By the time the environment is modelled, it has very often changed.

The computer, then, with all its wonderful technical abilities, is mostly used on the routine clerical and accounting work, on which, for the reasons shown earlier and later on, is often more expensive than the old, manual way. This might not be so if the computer were better suited to the world, or the world to the computer. Let us try to imagine an ideal computer system.

An airline systems manager once described what he saw as the ideal computer: no apparent input, no apparent output, the computer humming quietly away, and aircraft taking off, flying, and landing, all under its control. Near ideal as this is, there might be a better one, on the lines of the caveman's model drawing. That would be one with all a company's or society's, resources contained on it, with input from the environment, and output to it, where the high-priest controller stood in front of the console adjusting the environment as he saw fit.

If he wants more rain, he makes more rain, if he wants fewer coconuts, he makes fewer. Theoretically, and even possibly in the future, technically, it is possible to build such an ecological or environment control system, and it is certainly what every dedicated computer man wants to do with his computer in the company where he is employed. There are one or two large problems, however, and they are common to all computers.

Ignoring what is perhaps the biggest problem, that of constructing a model of such infinite variability and flexibility, there is still the enormous problem of capturing the input, the single problem that makes computers so expensive today.

The ideal computer would have to have cameras that automatically record every event in units of data that represent *controllable* event units. A device that measures the number of vehicles that pass in a traffic control system, manages to pick up events in controllable data units. The data units gathered are input to a system that can send back meaningful output action instructions. Such devices are possible where the events are amenable to automatic recognition, and a spectacular example is the input from space vehicles. The input goes down to the computer, automatically, and the corrective output signal comes back up.

But the only way that the ideal computer could capture data from the world of business and general operations would be one still to be invented. It would have to have a camera that recorded, not only the event, but the event by type and in required data units.

With present computer systems, humans participate in *translating* their event into an *input model* of that event—onto a piece of paper that will be key punched, read by an optical scanner, by keying in what they are doing, or have done, onto a terminal keyboard, and so on. The drawback is that this is very expensive. The computer-based information system needs its input in certain data signals if it is to be an accurate control model of reality, but the real events are not so easily translated into these data signals. The data model of the event, of course, by no means tries to represent all of the attributes; only those relevant attributes such as number, value and so on, are extracted. Generally, though, even these have to be written down.

If we stretch our imaginations and think of future or science fiction systems where such input recording would be a thing of the past, we could perhaps imagine a department store, where the shelves themselves registered the lifting off of goods by number, like a weighing scales, and where customers' fingerprints at the counter terminal designated the credit account to be charged. Such a system, unlikely as it might seem, is more feasible than any using voice recordings or films, so variable are the possibilities with these two.

Whether or not computer systems are economically feasible, a point we have promised to look at again later on, their development seems to be towards the ideal system with terminals proliferating and computers tending to be larger and more centralised. Ideal, as this may be, hardware-wise or cost-wise, it raises some enormous problems, chiefly the one mentioned earlier of knowledge loss. If it was upsetting to see knowledge and files pass to our own computer, or our nearest friendly computer centre, imagine it all going to one big central, government-based information utility.

Let us look at what could be transferred, in theory at least: all business processing, all utilities processing, communications switching, television and radio, libraries and educational systems, and so on.

One thing seems clear. Change in the world will have to be

greatly reduced if such centralised information systems are to be maintained. Looking at the exponential growth of information since the early nineteenth century, it seems reasonable to suppose that a new age of non-change, or permanence, is possible, particularly as it can be based on the certainty of computer technology, and particularly on the use of computer-based environmental, or ecological, control systems.

10 *using the computer*

The first step in deciding whether one should or should not use a computer is to obtain a *policy directive* to investigate the question. Simple as this may seem, it is often far from that, as the computer is an excellent device for passing the buck.

A computer can have one or two possible meanings for a senior manager who regards it only in terms of its political consequences for him. Firstly, it can make or break him within the company; secondly, if he is young enough or flexible enough, it may allow him to move as a senior manager with computer expertise outside the company. Taking the latter first, there is no greater myth than that of the senior manager with a knowledge of how computers affect company operations: all such a man can know is how a computer affected his company.

He will probably have been completely removed from all technical decisions. Other companies, about to get computers, however, will see him as a most desirable man, who can 'deal with the specialist'. In fact, he does everything the specialists tell him to do, and therefore, can be a very useful adjunct to the computer department. Which poses the thought that if every department had properly trained and motivated people, the best top management would consist of puppets. Inter-department rivalry could be fought out even more democratically through them, and eventually they could be disposed of quietly.

But to come back to things that are our business: the first kind of senior manager, who sees the computer only in terms of making or breaking him. He may simply want to steer clear of it altogether and pass the decision to a younger or more courageous man. He may want to grasp the nettle himself because he feels that it is the means of making him. Or, he may do what most politically minded senior managers do: try to have it both ways. Now we will try to describe this very complex set of steps, in what has to be a confused top management environment.

The first essential for such a manager, well known to the computer salesman, is to *avoid at all costs* being the one who advocates that the computer should be used. He will be around then, of course, larger than life, talking computers and technology, but ensuring that the decision has been transferred to an interdepartmental steering committee of some kind. If that is not possible, an even better tactic is to get oneself transferred to a different department, or group, at the time the computer is signed for and then get transferred back around the post-mortem stage when everyone else is blamed. If all that fails, there is even the ploy of being away ill during the critical feasibility stage.

With so many possibilities, added to the possibility that a careerist may have simply railroaded the computer in and then departed, it is not surprising that some companies drift into computer projects with no policy directives whatsoever.

To start with there should be a policy directive from the top, from the president or general manager. Who then should be appointed to appraise the project?

We saw that if any manager at any level was appointed and subsequently became head of the computer project, he might transfer his allegiance to himself and the computer industry. What if we give the decision to a manager who will *not* be in charge of the project? The big drawback is that he can now propose the impossible and afterwards claim that he himself could have made it work, or he can be careless and disinterested in what he is proposing. With the proviso that, despite this, a good senior manager may make this alternative a better proposition than the first, let us look at one other possibility.

Get external advice. There is no doubt that this is the best course of action, if the external adviser is good, and obviously not trying to land customers into a facilities service operation. The external adviser, for example, might suggest having a small computer rather than a big one, or using a service bureau, or even accounting machines. Who is this external adviser? Much as the author would like to include a list, it would reflect his bias, his social and business environment, and his own business interests. What follows, however, will give some guidance to the manager.

After the policy directive when a project leader has been appointed (this title does not automatically mean that there will be a computer project) the project *feasibility study* can take place.

With whole books dedicated to the subject of systems appraisal, planning and design, we will merely pick out the elements of each systems stage that are of interest to the senior manager.

The most vital element in the feasibility study is what is called the *cost-benefit analysis*. This must be considered apart from:

Possible future savings.
Philosophical considerations of entering the computer age.
Non-measurable increases in efficiency.

This is a cost analysis that should be based on reasonable timings—that is, how long each computer run will take. There are ways of calculating such timings, written about by this writer in detail elsewhere (*Installing and managing a computer*, Brandon Press, Business Books), but one good way is to ask an outside expert who knows not only how long a certain job should take to run, but how long similar jobs actually take to run on other people's computers. There is no better rule.

It is also very important to make sure that the cost-benefit analysis includes those manual, or clerical, costs that will continue after the computer system goes on the air, and these can be easily overlooked. On the benefit side, it is not enough to just add up the cost of clerks or operators saved. One must consider if the number of such people will really be reduced, or whether the company will keep them on until their retirement.

One must also ensure that each person is made completely replaceable by the system, especially if staff are working on a decentralised basis in small offices. If most of one man's work in a small office is taken away, and he is still needed to do the bit that is left, he must still be kept. You can reduce a staff force from one hundred to twenty in a centralised office by cutting down the work to one-fifth, but you cannot make such a reduction with forty offices.

If it is found to be economically feasible to use a computer, a model should be chosen that allows growth in *reasonable stages*. It is best to say what this does not mean. As we saw earlier the pay-off obtained by increasing memory and storage capacities and speeds is often so slight compared to the costs of such increases that the smallest reasonably effective upward step is another computer. Effective as that might be, it is not a reasonable economic solution. One of the greatest untruths in the computer industry is that certain computer models can grow in speed and capacity by adding reasonably priced processing blocks. A good rule for small to medium computers is that the cost of the effective minimum increase is often equal to the cost of another computer.

Two very important considerations in choosing a particular computer system are the languages and software to be used and future conversions to new computers. One should aim for a language like COBOL and avoid those languages and software that are tied to a specific manufacturer. One should also try to identify those extra 'free' routines a manufacturer may include with his version of COBOL as they also can tie him to a company. A choice of a universal language like COBOL also helps a company to make the inevitable change to a new system when it comes about. In choosing hardware, one must always ask how long any piece will be on the market in making a decisionto use it.

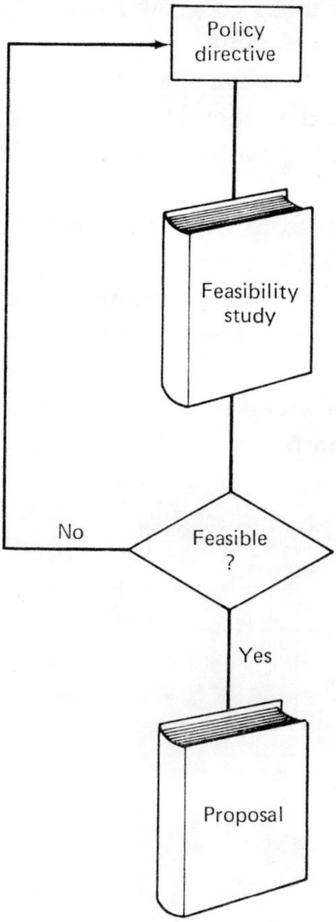

All of these considerations should be reflected in the feasibility study which follows the policy directive and which precedes the proposal.

Most of the work at the proposal stage can be done by the manufacturers who will want to supply their own proposals. Complete dependence upon them, which is very common at this stage, will lead straight to all the evils described earlier. Use of their proposals, however, can be very convenient for checking out timings and prices. A good rule is to add 25 per cent to the timings of all runs, both those done by the manufacturer and oneself. Every run tends to grow in size and complexity immediately after the proposal.

Many companies manage the first steps of policy directive, feasibility study, and proposal, and then let the project drift towards the inevitable post-mortem. The next stages are just as vital.

One could go on from here with page after page of plans, but we will leave that to the textbooks mentioned and continue instead at the management, personnel and environmental level —in other words, the real world in which all these plans have to operate.

The first thing we can say about systems planning, which must precede, accompany and succeed the project that merely

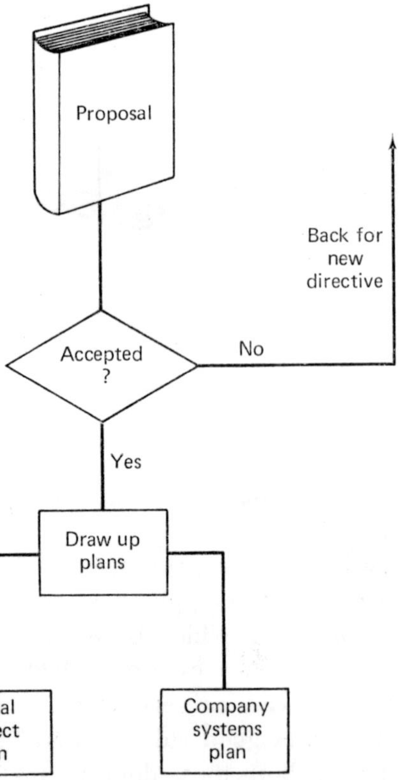

gets the computer in and initial jobs on, is that unless it is removed from the line organisation of the computer department it may become subordinated to the problems of the daily computer processing job. An important exception to this is where a senior manager has a continued interest in systems planning. If no one at the top is interested, the systems planners in the computer department will give up writing plans that nobody reads and begin to write books that might make money instead.

Another strong argument for moving systems planning away from the computer is that if it and systems analysis stay there, they might find themselves one of two systems planning groups, the other being the planning or operations research department. We noted earlier the different nature of these two systems jobs, one being concerned with the repetitive data-processing work, the other with the adaptive one-off probes.

There is a good case for removing the systems planning and analyses team altogether from the computer department and merging them with the research or planning group, as will be seen in a moment when we discuss the need to build an information system that does justice to both the control and adaptive needs of the business.

The strongest argument against such a move is that people who do not work in computer departments know nothing about computer systems. This is borne out by the fact that no other department can ever argue with the computer department about things that concern the computer, because it could never win.

One way around this that should solve some other problems, temporarily at least, is to promote the systems planning manager out of the computer department, even if he was top man there, and to promote all of the systems planning and analyses, or design, staff from there also, with the exception of specialists brought in to handle research and development or special planning techniques.

With such an organisation one could plan for an information system that would supply both the control and adaptive needs of a company. Very little can be said in a book like this about this extremely complex subject which is not even done justice in systems books; however, for the benefit of those interested in the subject we will say that all research and planning work is done by relating the company to the environment. Models of both can be constructed and manipulated from time to time, with the normal information systems supplying the basic elements that go into the company model. Much of the planning work, however, will be based not only on new possibilities, but

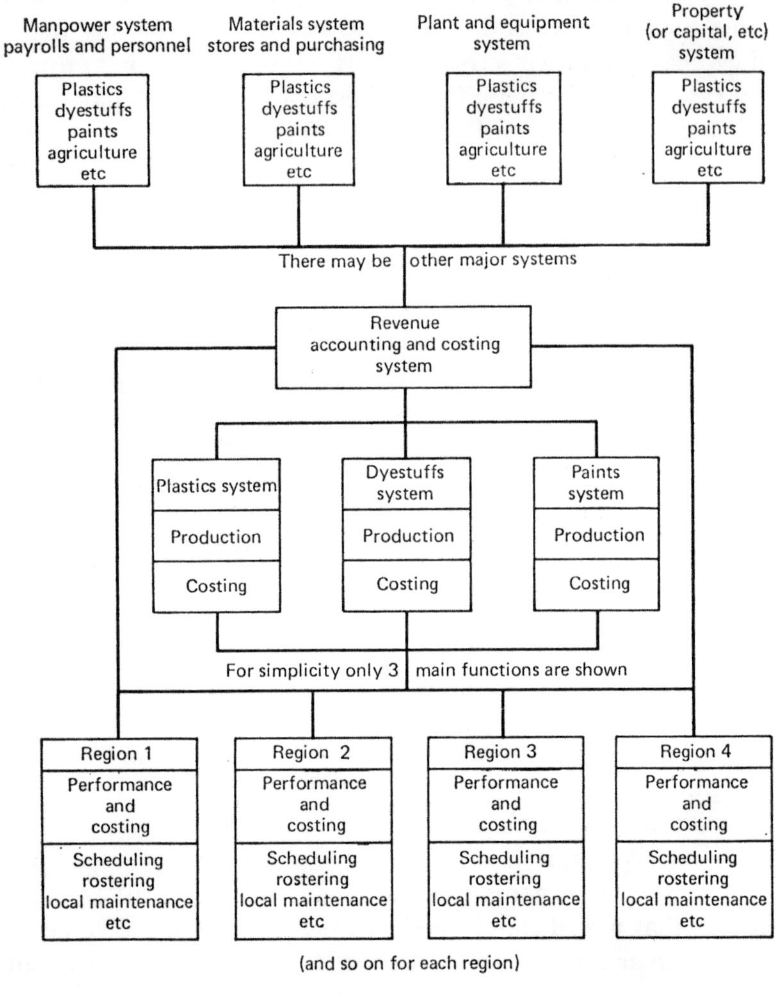

on past happenings or events; therefore, the information system must log the key transactions or events. In many cases this means every event—what was sold, where, to whom, by whom, and in what season.

As one can imagine, this is the most neglected kind of computer work. The computer department consists of hardworked

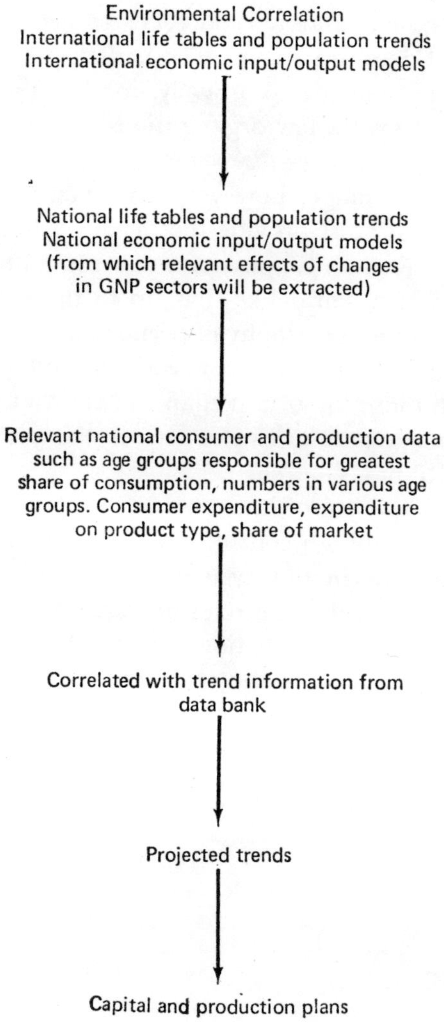

data processors. The research and development and other planning people talk grandly about models of the environment, but seldom look at *happenings*, how one is doing in bread or potatoes in a particular area at a particular time.

One reason for the success of the Roman Catholic Church is its excellent main product of salvation. Another very important reason is that it has managed to maintain a centralised information system and a rigidly centralised control policy, despite its vast decentralisation. The bad effects of decentralisation alone are enough to gravely inhibit the growth and efficiency of all save a few organisations which have dogmatic central policies.

In an age of change, however, a relevant control and information system must provide the means of both control and adaption. In a Roman Empire environment of no technological change, or even a world like that up to the early nineteenth century, a Platonic philosophy of permanence and rigid central policy are vital. In the modern world at times the ability to change seems more important than the ability to maintain the central control system, as can be seen in the trials and tribulations of the Roman Church.

Meanwhile, this era of intense change demands information systems that allow both control and adaptation. The last two pages show an information system that can be adjusted to suit most enterprises, and some relevant environmental indicators that can be used in conjunction with the logged events of the enterprise for adaption to the environment.

11 *the computer people*

Programmers are so hard to get and considered to be so important that at least one US company has given up wooing them in its advertisements and insults them just to be different. If you want to know about the golf and water-skiing and so on down here, the advertisement says about the famous holiday area the company is in, get in touch with the local chamber of commerce, don't bother us.

As the advertisement has appeared a few times, it probably works, especially with the American programmer who likes this kind of direct approach. Most of the other US companies, however, treat the prospective programmer employee as he is treated in Europe, as someone to be flattered, wooed and won.

If you're not happy with your job, one advertisement says, there's a way out, and it shows a large picture of a programmer going out through a door marked EXIT. In other words, we know that you are the most independent person in the world. Another advertisement asks for people with minds like Kant but broad enough for science fiction, while another, showing a picture of a little black ghetto girl, offers programmers and systems analysts a chance to help make the world a better place to live in. Is it any wonder that computer people feel superior?

One reason why the computer industry manages to employ so many good people is that it changes and expands so rapidly that intelligent and energetic people are given the opportunity to move towards and into the centres of highest development. Through good judgment they quickly reach positions of authority and, in turn, hire other intelligent people, so that the process magnifies itself. There is no sign of this process ending until the computer industry settles into bureaucratic stagnation like certain public utilities.

Another important reason is that it offers the adventurous and talented immense potential for self-fulfilment and advancement. It is well known that job enrichment is a very high motivating factor in work: the computer industry proves it to be far more effective than either authority or artificial industrial psychology. Such an environment can bring out the worst as well as the best in people, however, and even though the industry seems to bring out the best in them most of the time, the worst warrants recognition and rejection.

And the worst is perhaps the sense of superiority it creates in some, which borders on contempt for the non-computer man. It seems to be worse in Europe than in the US, and it is manifested particularly in certain 'computer society' groups. Computer society courses and new university-based computer courses heavily bolster their syllabuses with mathematical and pseudo-scientific techniques. To look at some courses and computer society journals one would think that most, if not all, of work with computers was supported by a knowledge of Boolean algebra, mathematical equations, and operations research techniques. Such subjects have played an important part in the production of computer systems and software, and in certain uses of computers, but *not* in their normal use. Most of the uses of computers in the world are in commercial work as is witnessed by the thousands of advertisements in the magazines for programmers.

One can take up a computer society journal and go through it from cover to cover and not find a single paper about the design and management of commercial computer-based information systems, or the programming of such systems in the way that they are actually programmed. From cover to cover the papers will describe exotic techniques that may be seldom used *to any significant advantage* to a computer user.

The hard, plain facts are that most work that uses a computer in the English-speaking world is in English, and that most programming work, perhaps more than 90 per cent, needs no more mathematics than a knowledge of addition and subtraction. No matter what excuses are put forward by universities and computer societies, their aims should be chiefly to support the user, especially in the case of the computer society, where nearly every member has the food he eats and the clothes on his back paid for by a commercial employer-computer user. If most of the work is in English and simple arithmetic, some of the contents of the computer society journals must be assumed to be technological padding.

What is in short supply in courses and such journals is information on good project planning, systems planning, methodologies of work, proper standards and security, and, above all, management information and plain, good accounting for profit or loss. How can people be trained to design and implement computer-housed management information and control systems, if they are never trained in management information systems, or in even the rudiments of accounting and business?

What do we find when we look at computer education? The first thing is that there is an enormous business being carried on by private programming schools who sell courses in what can only be described as a perverse confidence trick. Exploiting the hopes of thousands of under-educated, and often unendowed, young people, they advertise through pictures of the glamorous computer world, where they claim that anyone who passes an aptitude test can make the grade.

For a start, there is no check on the validity of these aptitude tests nor on the results or how they are applied. These schools are in business for profit, for the sales of courses, and have neither legislation nor educational authorities to inspect or control them. Computer managers all over the western world constantly receive requests for advice from young people who are paying money in the process of taking a course. It is plain to these managers that most of the enquirers, having neither the education nor the aptitude, are being exploited.

When such schools first began in the late fifties in the United States, they were usually run in night classroom courses. They were filled with the young people who were the most likely targets, who, through either having dropped out from school or being unable to finish school, were now inspired by the promise of quick and easy success. With little written about computer science or programming at the time, the courses were given by programmers and punched card machine specialists, who were hired by the schools to teach in their spare time. Even if a young person had ability, his chances of getting a job afterwards were very slim, as his diploma was more likely to count against, rather than for him.

If that seemed unfair, consider that at the time computers were being introduced into a world still dominated by clerical labour. Many of these clerks were highly experienced and trained. There were the ones being tested by employers, and recruits who had finished high school and university. Also at the time, training was being given free to computer users by the manufacturers, so that no computer manager paying out hundreds of thousands of dollars for a computer system was too interested in someone having paid two or three hundred dollars for a doubtful night course. Those managers who were interested in giving everyone a chance soon became disillusioned by the quality of the people who held such diplomas.

As the industry advanced into the sixties and seventies, the form of the courses changed. One great disadvantage of the night classroom courses was that the customer saw what the other customers were like and began to realise that he was being trained with people who did not look like the intelligent programmers in the advertisements; also it became dishonourable for programmers to earn money at night by leasing themselves to the school entrepreneurs. By then, however, written material was becoming available and a billion dollar business began in home study course.

The home study course has several enormous advantages for

the organisers over all other forms of course. First, and foremost, it is impossible to finish, as one cannot go through a programming course alone and without a computer nearby to program one's way to understanding. As computers became more complex, it became vital for the trainee to work in a team, where his fellows and seniors could help him, and where the hardware was nearby. For the private schools, however, this problem was a major breakthrough, for the would-be programmer with no one else to communicate with, and working on a course that had a natural built-in failure device, would never finish the course, assume that the failure was within himself, and, thus, never come back waving his diploma, claiming that he could not get a job, and demanding his money back. Some of the private schools employed good standards from the start, a few even attained full acceptance in the US and deservingly flourished; but the great majority exploited a gullible customer market. These last are doing even better today than ever before.

The other chief source of computer education up to recent times was the manufacturers, who gave training to the staff of those companies who purchased or rented their machines. This training was reasonably good, although strictly limited to the jobs of programming and computer implementation.

In recent times a boom has begun for anyone in the computer education market, a boom that was helped by manufacturers' decision to begin charging for services like education that had been free formerly. Computer consultants, software houses, and independent course writers like this author, began to produce courses for industry and universities, and even, in cases where the people who gave the course could supply hands-on computer training, for the public. The public is still largely taboo, however, to the computer professional, because of the stigma attached to sales of courses in this area.

Courses to companies became a big market. There were two kinds, chiefly: first the 'flesh and blood' seminar type classroom course where a teacher was used, and then the self-study course, from manuals, programmed test, or audio-visual devices.

Most of them continued to suffer from the one grave defect: over-emphasis on business information and control systems. This neglect, however, merely serves to highlight a larger weakness in the education of most computer people, a weakness that could have a significant and serious effect on the world which they are bringing into being.

The sad truth is that most computer people are uneducated. They are intelligent, highly-motivated, positive and well-meaning people, but they are literally programming social systems based on 'truth machines' in a world they make no attempt to understand. They are, in fact, programming new control models of reality that range over government, industry and the social scene, models that incorporate social science.

With the physical sciences leaping ahead of the social, by perhaps fifty years or more, it is an understatement to say that the architects of society need urgent training in the humanities; and yet, the computer industry is dominated by graduates with physical science backgrounds.

If we consider two of the major issues of our times, those of the privacy and freedom of the individual, and education, we will realise that computers are drastically affecting both. There is no place in this book for a discussion of either, for they are treated extensively elsewhere, and this author is expressing his views on the second in another book which he has been re-writing for some time; what must be stressed here, though, is that computer people are generally ill-equipped to comment on either of these two issues of our age.

We look at the academic and literary worlds for commentators to pass judgment, or offer opinions, on what the computers will do to our civilisation, and we find either a total silence on the matter, or utterly extraordinary statements of the obvious. One sometimes feels that computers must have been planted here by people from outer space, we know so little about them. And we are so busy losing money misusing them that we have not thought about their most obvious use: as inventory and control systems of nature's resources and mankind's use of them.

Perhaps we must wait until training in computer science becomes one more subject on the school syllabus, rather than an education in itself. And this is what is beginning now. Some consultants advertising new computer courses for schools say that the school child of the future 'must be able to read, write and program'. What he is being taught, however, although immensely better than nothing, falls far short of what is required that he should be taught, which is surely the place of control systems in the history of man, from the caveman's wall painting down through the data systems of Mesopotamia, to an explanation of computer-housed data systems in the modern world.

Imagine, how easily a child grasps the concept of a real-time system with terminals. The caveman-manager stabs the control model: the beast falls outside; the program in the central processor registers the action condition, sets off channel action, activates the refinery process, traffic signal, or space ship, as the case may be. Imaginative examples, eagerly grasped by a child, far better than computer manufacturer's descriptions of their hardware.

Above all, though, what may be lacking in the computer education of the young is education in the basic fact of classification, the methodology of gathering, storing, labelling and accessing information in the world, so vital in an age of exploding information, and so vital to the education of the young facing a world in which a multitude of subjects must be classified.

How would this writer decide the school syllabus of one of the computer architects of the new world? Not with physics or engineering or science courses, although they are certainly needed by the architects of the new computer hardware. If he is to be a social systems engineer or systems analyst designing business or economic or urban computer-based systems, he should be educated in the history of information systems and management science, a history that takes him from the urban revolution down through the medieval world to Watt and Boulton and to today. He should be educated in classification and information retrieval techniques, and, above all, in liberal arts, the most neglected subjects of all in the computer industry today.

If one should search through a computer centre for a person interested in liberal arts, the low-paid and largely uneducated key-punch group of teenage girls is where he should spend his time, for it is there that he is most likely to find a book lover, or someone interested in drama or art, although exceptions can be found in female programmers. The well-intentioned male computer professional simply does not take the time to consider what motivates the masses of people outside his computer centre, or how they are going to adjust to the kind of world he is bringing about. When they start to throw rocks at the windows of his computer centre it may be too late for him to find out what is going on.

12 *the computer market*

It is not until we look at the state of the market for people that we begin to realise the full consequences of the myth-to-post-mortem cycle we looked at earlier. Imagine that we have gone through that cycle in one, or even more than one, company and now, wiser and more experienced, we are associated with a new company about to install its first computer. In other words about to enter its age of idealism.

These days it will have to have a large clerical force from which programmers can be selected through aptitude tests and trained if it is to get started at all and it will have to get enough experienced people from outside to act as senior programmers and team or project leaders.

There are two ways to get more than the normally available quota of experienced people: the first is by offering unusually high salaries; the second by going for the most advanced and sophisticated hardware possible. Although the second is enormously more expensive than the first, the first does the most harm to the whole industry by inflating salaries and increasing staff turnover.

Even without the attractions of higher salary, some experienced staff would be available anyway, due to the normal reasons of insufficient promotional possibilities where they are, and the desire to get away from whatever set of programs they have been stuck with, so that if no company offered more pay most of them would get some experienced staff through advertising, except those that have a bad image or an unpleasant product or location. It is never like that in practice, of course, so salary offers continue to spiral.

Let us assume then that by offering higher salaries than others, and by announcing exciting plans for sophisticated hardware, our new company gets more than an adequate supply of experienced outside help and enters its age of idealism. Like the first company we looked at in our first chapters, the computer staff of this one is made up in the usual reasonable manner:

An over-all experienced manager.
Some senior experienced people.
A large number of younger inside people.
A few not so young inside people.

As we saw earlier, dissent may arise amongst some or all of the last category from the start, but there is no need to go into this passing phase again, except to remark that with every year that passes these phases may happen faster.

After the first two years, just as the initial stages of jobs are going onto the air, the younger 'insiders' begin to leave, grateful to the company that has trained them and to the experienced senior staff that have helped them along, but determined to leave anyway, in some cases even in the face of equal and higher pay offers than those in the new jobs. The exact reason will be looked at in a moment, but let us follow the process through first.

For some time the older insiders, with the usual few notable exceptions, of course, continue to grumble about the experienced staff being against them, the management being against them, and life being against them, absolutely ignoring the fact, on the surface, at least, that their younger colleagues are moving up and out past them. When they do comment on this staff loss, they blame the company for not paying the highest market rate to keep them, and paying themselves even more.

Eventually staff losses from the younger inside group reach such proportions that management decides to recruit from outside. The moment they make this decision they face up to the possible consequences of such action, which are that if they bring in experienced staff they will set off a wave of resignations from

1 The rest of the younger insider people.
2 Some of the senior insider and outsider group.

And they will very much increase the complaints from the older insider group.

Under these circumstances they do the only thing they can, which is start recruiting trainees again, the only course of action which will not annoy anybody, and sensible in the light of spiralling market salaries and market demand. At this stage, however, because of the lead time required to advertise for, select and train programmers, the company can only hope that staff losses will ease off. They do not, of course; if anything they increase, until, soon, nearly all of the original younger staff, recruited from within are gone, and the experienced outside people are also beginning to leave.

Around this time the true ability of a company to respond with intelligence to the needs of its computer become apparent. If top management merely sits at the controls of what is an established utility type or drifting enterprise, and is incapable of facing up to the kind of situation we are describing (one which we have promised to explain shortly), nearly *all* of the good young people from within and *all* of the experienced people hired from outside will leave.

If management is wise enough to respond along the lines mentioned in the earlier chapters, by accepting systems plans and recruiting trainees to the *point* of *over-recruitment*, they may manage to hold together a reasonable computer operation; but, and here is the crux of the matter, regardless of what kind of top management is in charge, development will be severely curtailed. And this is because of market growth rates.

Imagine a perfectly happy and harmonious computer department working under a loved and competent top management. After three years, say, the position might be as follows.

20 mostly good young programmers with 3 years experience.
4 senior programmers.
8 systems analysts, half promoted from young programmers, half older men.
2 managers.
1 over-all project manager.

Now place this harmonious computer department into the current computer industry environment, into the United States, Japan or any of about ten European countries. Let us pick a country with 1,000 computers. In the year that we are observing our harmonious computer department, the growth rate will cause the number of computers to increase by anything up to 1,500. The 500 new computer users will also select and train new programmers from within, but they will hire experienced people as senior staff from outside, from the 1,000 companies, yes, but *especially from the big successful user* who has reached the stage we have described.

So success is the chief cause of failure. No matter what the young programmers with three years' experience are paid, to stay with the first company, they will still be very strongly attracted by the thought of more senior jobs elsewhere, as systems analysts, say, or senior programmers in charge of a small team. The better the company we have been considering, the more staff it will lose. A good company will lose most and possibly all of its good people, and find itself promoting the bad to stay on the air.

It is important to consider what stage has been reached in the company that experiences these losses. Initial capital outlay will have been as follows:

The cost of setting up the computer department and building.

The cost of the first one to two years of programming before any jobs went live.

For a medium-sized installation the first will run between six and eight hundred thousand dollars, the second four to five hundred thousand; that is over a million dollars in original capital outlay before any savings can be achieved.

Around the third year, the computer department of the size pictured will be running at a cost of something over one million a year. As the staff replaced by the system are probably still around, this million will at first appear as additional on the expenditure side of the financial accounts, and indeed should really be charged as part of the initial capital outlay until the system breaks even.

Let us imagine that our computer department is one of the very few that manages to get rid of whatever people the computer has replaced, or has managed to affect immediate increases in efficiency, so that it breaks even in the third year. Note that there is no question of an average commercial computer department doing any better than breaking even at this stage.

The hard work is now over. Forty analysts and programmers have been hired, created and welded into a design and implementation team that have raised a new building, learned systems and programming, built the beginnings of a computer-based information and control system, and, most important of all, learned something about the company and how it works.

At this vital, three-year stage, the company can now use this large group of trained computer systems specialists *to achieve savings* in further development. But by then staff losses have begun and are quickly reaching the stage where all development halts. The manager spends his time deploying his forces to cover maintenance and security. Trainees are hired, but by now it is certain that at their two- and three-year stages, just when they could begin to understand systems, they also will leave to install other companies' computers.

Why has this company bought this computer the manager asks? Has it made an outlay of over a million dollars so that it could lose hundreds of thousands of dollars a year, or at best break even? Is this the price of staying with it? Or is it all an elaborate myth? He cannot be blamed for asking these questions, which we will try to answer later on.

This is the predicament of the manager of the well run computer department, in the face of staff losses, but while he is reporting this desperate situation up to the top, he may be aware that if he did have the staff that he would have to face up to two other evils already mentioned: diminishing processing and storage capacity, diminishing available processing time. The only reasonable verdicts are the following.

All the signs of the market for the next ten years are that users will contantly lose their experienced programmers to newer users. The usual counter move against this, which is to hire trainees, merely puts one into the programmer supply and placement business.

Therefore, potential computer users should be aware that at best all they will do is program and maintain certain initial projects for their computers, and not succeed in performing any further significant systems design. Commercial computer systems with a few exceptions, may for some years continue to be run at a loss, which may be considered the price of using this new technology.

For the potential computer user, however, the next trend is just as important. This is the process, briefly described earlier, of good people moving towards the centres of expertise and development. The really top-notch man will not stay with a company that handles its computer project badly. He will move to one that handles it better or to a computer software or facilities supply house. If he moves to the latter, he may take the best programmers with him, plus a contract to maintain the programs of the company where he was employed at a far higher price than that which was paid to him. The managers who are arranging this attempt to sooth their conscience by saying that it is easier to pay him fifty thousand a year as an outside adviser than to get permission to raise his salary by one thousand as an employee.

Once he gets the contract, for his own company or for the facilities company he has joined, he is well on the road to getting more contracts and programmers. One advertisement to programmers from such a company recently asked, 'Is your boss a professional computer man?' (Implying that he might be an impostor manager, which many computer managers are); 'If he is not, why not pack up and come to work with us where we are all real computer people right up to the top?'

Now let us think about the implications of that adverisement. It is really saying to the programmer, leave your non-technical boss because there is no reason to carry him. Come to us, and because you've walked out on him, he'll have to give us his business. Presumably, and hopefully, they will smile at the non-technical customer at that stage.

The market trends are leading computer users straight into the arms of the facilities suppliers and consultants. There are two main avenues: the first via the post-mortem through consultants, the second by letting out more and more programming work as time goes on. In both cases, the computer user becomes more firmly caught up in a technical web that he may never withdraw from.

No one wants to face the truth. Managers will spend more money to buy off consultants with promises of more work to keep them quiet. The consultants, delighted with a market situation in which the computer user is confused and mystified, smile and say, 'Ah, yes, you are in trouble: you need us'.

Top management is not going to say that it has spent a couple of million for nothing. It is much easier to talk about future benefits and great new future technological possibilities.

The outside programming service and facilities supplier gets more and more business. As there are not enough computer programmers to go around anyway, he must steal from his potential customers. This he does with increasing ease, for he is in the computer selling business, and he offers the programmers an environment where they mix with their fellows and share in profits.

If we follow this possible trend through to its conclusion we will see that the computer user could end up having paid millions for a computer system that does not pay, paying far more than he had to pay before he lost his programmers to have his computer programmed, and possibly even operated. He could thus be in a position of paying for something he no longer controls or even understands.

Let us now look down the list of beneficiaries. We have the young programmers, picked out from their dull clerical jobs and given a chance of an exciting and highly paid career, which most of them grasp. In the three-year period we described, it is possible for a programmer, starting as a trainee at the beginning of it, to end up with his salary doubled.

Next, we have the software, consulting and facilities supply people. Above all these are the ones making their fortunes. We need just remind ourselves that some of the world's records in fast fortunes have been broken here by such people in recent years. And we might also remember that the business of these people is *not* using computers for business, but *helping* business people to use computers.

There are many more, as we showed earlier, but apart from the omnipotent ones behind it all, these two groups are the main beneficiaries. And as for number one, read the next chapter.

13 *we all work for the manufacturer*

There is an old and untrue saying that the man that pays the piper calls the tune. The computer user pays the computer manufacturer, who is the chief piper, but the piper calls the tune much of the time. A senior computer manufacturer executive was once reported as saying that it was not important to make the right decision, but what was important was to make the decision right.

This philosophy is only too clear when one looks at the computer industry, where the computer manufacturer is so powerful that his customers and their companies must at times adapt to suit him. So great is the power and influence of the manufacturer that in some cases he even pays for user associations that are composed of thousands of users who get together to discuss how to program, install, and manage the hardware they rent or buy from him.

If he ever had any fear that such large groups of users would turn against him, he no longer has, for they have been known to vote overwhelmingly against any motion to discuss or examine his contracting or pricing methods. When one sees such user groups in action, however, one realises that members have more than their admiration for, and loyalty to, the manufacturer to help them make such a vote of confidence. They also have the welfare of the computer industry at heart.

So, other user groups come into being, with the prime purposes of advising their members in their dealings with the manufacturer and demanding that rate increases be given prior considerations. The more successful of these groups manage to get interest and intervention from governments. In virtually every case though, a few unthanked managers carry much of the total burden of such efforts, only getting other users to join out of their sense of shame. There is no sense in going into it here, for the facts are plain throughout the computer industry: computer people tend to care only about their own profession.

The manufacturer sets the pace in hardware development with the philosophy that what is new must be better than what has gone before, regardless of what development cost has been incurred to implement the old, and what will be needed for the new. Any illusions that the user has the freedom to ignore such developments must be dispelled immediately for the user has absolutely no choice but to accept, purchase and install the newly developed hardware.

If he does not, his old hardware, or 'old generation' may not be supported by the manufacturer, and, whether that happens or not, his programmers will leave him, as programmers will not stay with out-dated hardware, unless new hardware is contracted for and scheduled for a date in the foreseeable future.

Much has been learned now about the trials and tribulations of moving from one generation of computers to the next, but, although more preparation can be made now with this new knowledge than before, there is no guarantee that the conversion will be any less painful or costly. In fact, such a conversion at this stage could be a disaster for many users, but more about that after we look more closely at this whole development process.

Needless to say, the manufacturer must develop; if he did not he would hardly stay in business, as his competitors would leave him behind. The extent and rapidity of his developments, however, are functions of:

His control of the market.
His ability to lead his customers.

His own ability to meet the demands that he is creating within his own enterprise and outside.

When a manufacturer releases a new generation of computers, all users must change over as soon as possible, for the reasons already given. This means that much and, very often, *all* of their development must be halted while they attend to this changeover. This enormous expense, of course, is justified on the grounds that the new, more expensive, generation will give faster throughput, greater capacity and so on. It gives all these certainly, but at correspondingly higher costs.

Meanwhile, the all-important development effort is being channelled into an activity that will simply result in the user running hard, to stay in the same place. The transfers or conversions from the early generation computers were so bad that one shudders to think of what it is going to mean with some of the large systems of today.

What does it mean to make such a conversion? It means taking all your programs and files off the computer that you have and making them work on a bigger, newer, and faster one.

You begin by installing the new one long before you remove the old. How else can you do it? You pay for two computers, and will continue to pay for them for some time. There are several possible courses.

1 With slight adaptation, if you had been wise enough to use COBOL, say, you make your programs work on the new system, and then you convert your files.
2 If you cannot use your programs directly you must:
a Translate them using a translator if there is one.
b Simulate or emulate them on the new computer.
c Re-write them.

Daunting as the last possibility seems, it is often the only reasonable long-term solution, because the first two methods of translating or emulating can make your programs bigger and slower, so that they run on the new more expensive hardware at the same old speeds at a new price. It is ironical that the translation and emulation programs and hardware devices that cause you to use up more computer time and capacity, which you pay for according as you use it, are supplied by the manufacturer who is charging you for this hardware. *Ironical* here is stressed as there is no doubt that one cannot produce a translator or emulator that would make a program more efficient.

If you had been wise enough to use COBOL, it must be added that although this certainly makes you much better off than the people who did not use it, you do not escape the cost of conversions even with COBOL, for new versions of it may be announced every few years, and manufacturers may decide to support the new versions only.

Now this writer can think of no just reason why a manufacturer should discontinue supporting a programming language without giving about five years' notice. It could mean that a user is forced to change many of his programs to the new version. As he cannot spend all his time working hard to stay in the same place, and as he may not have the programmers for the conversion, he may be tempted to use another translator conveniently prepared by the manufacturer also. He should be aware, before using this, that this may also make his programs bigger and slower. If they get bigger they may 'bust core', that is, not fit in main working memory; if they get slower he may need more computer time. Translating programs the easy way could lead directly to purchasing more hardware.

We have been talking mostly about past conversions, but what of converting systems the size of today's? Imagine if a computer manager had some or all of the problems mentioned earlier and a new generation computer was announced. It may not happen for some time, and it may happen tomorrow. We have probably reached the stage where the manufacturers are aware of how such an announcement would be received by existing users, and yet the facts are that most of the people who will be users in five years' time do not have computers yet. They are the lucky ones who will not have the next conversion on their hands. If the manufacturers know that they will get their custom with a new generation, they might be prepared to suffer the agonies of the rest.

Another possibility is that the smaller manufacturer with no great *clientele* to worry about might decide to try a technological leap-frog over the bigger ones. Their response to that would certainly be a newer, bigger and faster model than his. Hopefully what we will see is the big manufacturer getting the best of both worlds, by bringing in what looks like and sounds like a new generation, but what can be regarded as an extension to the old.

Sound advice is not to oversimplify any conversion. The rule is not to get a computer if you think there might be a new generation or model around the corner. A better rule will be given later.

Even within generations, computers are plagued with hardware and, particularly, software modifications. For an easy understanding of 'software' in this sense consider it as the programs that make your programs work in the hardware.

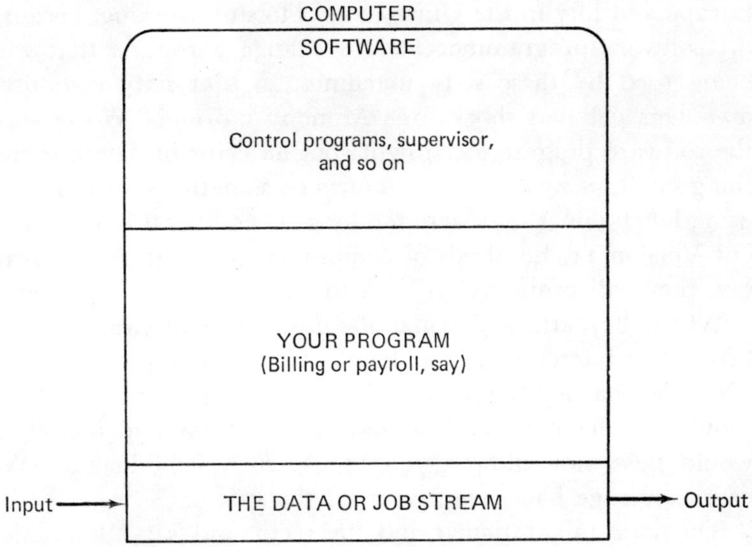

Each user has his software tailored to his particular hardware and programming languages. Some users have optical scanners and FORTRAN, for example, others have floating-point arithmetic and ALGOL. Despite the fact that each user's software is tailored to him, it comes to him from the manufacturer in versions with modifications. Let us call our software Titan and say that when we join the club our computer arrives with a Titan software package that is at Version 10.

We might be quite happy with Version 10, until some user in Japan decides to do something utterly ridiculous that no one else has ever done with some unusual hardware gadget or software routine, and hangs up in the process. He notifies the manufacturer who notices that Titan was not geared to handle this kind of activity, so he updates it and sends out modifications or 'patches' to all users to insert them if they wish. Finally when the modifications reach a certain number, he brings out a new version of Titan called Version 11, which incorporates all the changes since 10 including unusual ones like the one raised in Japan.

Now that Japanese change may cause ten computers in Europe and fifty in the United States to stop working, because the software programmer had to change a routine that was being used by these sixty machines, so that sixty computer managers get bad shocks one Monday morning. Worse still, the software programmer might spot an error in Titan, something say 'that was letting customers do something invalid', like using label names that were too long. If he fixes this and sends out Version 11, hundreds of computers may halt. Needless to say, they will promptly go back to Version 10.

When they attack the manufacturer, he will calmly reply, 'Your key names were too long'. They will reply, 'They've been like that for two years!' Back comes the response, 'They should not have been. Had our software not had a bug, it would have not allowed you to use such field lengths. We cannot change back now; we need the space'.

The user might then grind his teeth and say, 'I am not changing my programs. I will stay at Version 10'. The manufacturer will reply, 'In six months then we will discontinue to support your system'. The lesson appears to be: move on with the bandwagon or get off; there is no in between.

One or two big US companies have decided on the latter and stopped accepting software releases. One systems manager who made such a decision had a large system operating on what was almost a national scale with many terminal users. Some of these terminals were computers in their own right. A software conversion resulting in a bug on the main system could cause either the system to halt or jobs to be distorted at a number of terminal points.

Satisfied with the version he had, where bugs had settled to a reasonable level, the systems manager made the decision to freeze it and accept no more changes. He was such a big customer that it seemed certain that he would go on getting hardware maintenance support. It is certain that no manufacturer would refuse maintenance in any circumstances. If trouble did develop, however, he could point the finger at the manager who had refused to move on to new software releases and claim that the proper operation of the hardware was conditional on its operating under the latest software. There is no use looking for an arbitrator in such matters: the whole business is too complicated for any outsider to understand it.

The position then is that the computer user is helping to pay for an extraordinary new industry in which the seller and supporters are making fortunes. The computer profession's best salesmen are the computer managers and staff in every computer department. In many cases when the man who is paying the bill listens to his computer people, or to service and support groups, he might as well listen to a computer salesman, for they are often on his side. Everyone is making money, everyone getting fulfilment and making a better world, except the user who is paying for it.

Is it possible, however, that he deserves it? It is very possible that although he may not deserve it that he has to suffer it. Any manager that installed a computer into his company on the sort of terms mentioned in this book, and let it go through some of the worst processes discussed must face up to the facts that his world has changed to the point where he must pass control over to someone else, but to whom?

It may sound heretical but to who else except senior computer people? They will *not* be taken in by technological myths if they are at the top. Remember they do not authorise computers, but merely install them; their managers issue the authorisations. Certainly they may have been guilty of loyalty to the computer profession, but who can blame them if their companies did not care about how their computers were used.

But does the user deserve what happens, and can the worst be avoided by newcomers to the field? Many users deserve what happens to them. Without something as big and complex as a computer, they could have gone on muddling until their retirements. The computer, at least, separates the managerial sheep from the goats.

Would we be unkind to ask whether many managers can really manage. Here is a test. Let us say that we have an expensive computer that produces a lot of reports, few of which reach the top, and let us design some which we feel should reach the top. These will be in the MIS category, but, to avoid that abused term, let us simply call them management reports. We will suggest a most basic set, so often ignored—personnel reporting, derived from payroll.

We will propose a system through which management can see overtime and absence rates per department, related to a standard or average, and one that shows numbers employed in standard work units or assignments—for example, numbers of office cleaners. We can fairly easily predict the costs of such a system, but what about the payoff? We can only say that the payoff is *whatever use management makes of such information.* If management ignores it, or is incapable of appreciating it, forget about it.

If management is capable of such appreciation, a reporting system like the above could highlight important potential areas of activity for work study, industrial engineering and organisation and methods work. Which brings us face-to-face with an important, and much ignored, aspect of computer systems—they are *measuring devices* as much as control devices. They should serve work study and methods people rather than their own artificial and mystical technological ends. Every computer project should lead to re-organisation and new methods in the departments it affects.

No manager then should authorise a computer that will merely replace the routine accounting and clerical work, unless such a replacement promises real savings. If it does not, and no firm plans for more worthwhile projects materialise, there is a strong case for using devices that are not popular with computer professionals. The case for using small accounting machine type computers for jobs like stores and billing is often very strong. No good computer man likes to work with these key-driven machines as they are small and unsophisticated, lacking the ability to do many of the things that he never gets around to doing on his bigger computer.

They are cheap, however, and easy and fast to install; therefore, one avoids the large development costs associated with the bigger machine. The moment one moves from the small key-driven accounting machine computer, one enters the world of sophisticated programming and software and spends amounts of money and time on these *purely computer activities* that are out of all proportion to the cost of the systems and the expected savings.

This book is not advocating accounting machines instead of computers. It is saying that if you intend to get a computer, consider leaving certain jobs on accounting machines, if the loss in benefits to be achieved by using the computer is not too great; then do a cost-benefit analysis of the computer's application to new work.

On the other hand, if we want to be really mature and honest about the whole business of using computers in the commercial world, let us forget about such marginal savings as those achieved by putting jobs onto accounting machines, and let us sign for our computers using the only real justification, good old-fashioned progress.

No one is going to stop buying computers. Our ability to buy them and the manufacturers' ability to sell them will shortly be limited by the supply of experienced computer people available. Even the most eager customer will hardly sign on the dotted line if he cannot get someone to install what he buys. The suppliers of programming services may be the ones to shortly decide the speed at which computers continue to be sold.

The user will go on buying whether he has to get his computer programmed and operated outside or not, for the simple reason that computers, like the locomotive and jet plane, are here to stay whether one likes it or not. But can the user accept the conclusions to be drawn from this? Very few computers are economic propositions yet. When there are so many computers and programmers around that users get time to settle down and do some real systems work, they may become economic propositions; meanwhile, nearly every computer user in the world is paying for the computer revolution, putting computers into the world that posterity will benefit from. He is working for the computer manufacturer, the computer industry, and future computer users. If he wants a good rule it is that the longer he puts off getting his computer the greater his chances of using it to his advantage—that is, as long as all other potential users do not take up the same attitude.

14 *except those that work for ourselves*

What advice, then, can we give the manager who is attempting to assess the viability of a computer project? First he must ask how much of savings are based on staff savings and how much of these can be achieved within five years. Unless most of the staff saved are being transferred, fired or retired within the five years, most of the staff savings figure cannot be reached.

If these conditions apply, and if the significant justification for the computer is staff savings, there is a strong case for something other than a full-sized computer operation, such as a small computer with time-sharing terminal facilities. If one bears in mind the two trends of smaller computers and large central time-sharing computers, the emergence of terminals that happen to be both are extremely significant. The question for the doubtful potential user is whether there is a computer or computer device that will allow him to begin to use computer techniques without the kind of investment and overheads needed to run a full centre.

As for the many cases where it is clear that it is economically viable to use one's own medium rather than a large-scale computer, the judgment must be use it by all means. But for those users in present times the strong warning must be repeated that staff turnover can make even the most profitable computer unprofitable.

What about future trends? Only the *naïve* or mad would attempt to forecast what the future holds in an age of intense change. Even within the computer industry in ten years many forecasters have been proven wrong. At one time there was great talk about 'cybernetics' and machine intelligence, from academic people, of course, not from computer people who had to work for a living. Anyone who works with computer systems knows that the data system that he and his fellows program, is doing the controlling, not the computer, and that to talk of 'machine intelligence' is nonsensical.

Another foolish forecast was that the world was about to be engulfed in computer output—tons of reports pouring out on top of managers, drowning them in information. No such thing happened, of course, because who would be bothered reading such information when the systems can be programmed to do whatever the managers would do upon reading such reports?

Then there was the popular myth of the 'package program', the standard payroll, or billing or economic planning, or what have you, program, that you would buy and then adjust for your own conditions. Such packages would put programmers out of business. This very commonly held view, even in the computer business, shows that many people know even less about the world and the way it does its business than they know about computers. The immense variation and constant change of business and of life does not allow programming. Take the simplest of routines, like billing, say, and write a package program, which is open to adjustment by means of 'paramater cards'. You describe your particular kind of input, and the kind of bill you want to the program, and you also describe the customer profile or format you would like in your file.

The person you have to hire to do such a job needs to know so much about computers and programs to get the unwieldy package program to work the way you want it to work that he would be quicker writing his own specific purpose billing program.

Can we guess the trends though? We can only guess, but we can also speculate on what the most talked about one would mean to the world we inhabit. That is the trend towards bigger and more centralised computer systems, with users operating over terminals, in what is now known as *time-sharing mode*.

The same breathtaking decisions face the manager who thinks about this. Can he pass his company's files and part of his company's control system over to an outside company? Will user knowledge of the job be greater or less? User knowledge will be greater if the real *user*, the man for whom the job was originally programmed has access to the system over terminals, which is what time-sharing is supposed to be about.

This perhaps is the closest we may get to making computers work for us, especially if we can forego all the costs of installing our own computers in return for a reasonable time-sharing rental. If you think of the one million dollar initial capital figure we saw earlier and take out the amount that is spent on the special building and special work to do with each machine, that amount is available for higher rents on a time-sharing scheme over about a five-year period.

To this can be added the yearly costs of running one's own computer operation. It all remains to be proven by the future, however. We might have to go through some catastrophic losses of company information on the central system before this mode of operation is in to stay, and reasonable costs may have to await future new technology; it does seem, however, to be one good way of putting control back where it belongs—into the hands of the real users, the ones for whom the jobs are being run.

So to some extent at least this may be the world of the future—bigger, centralised computers, increasing amounts of information passing to the central computer files, more and more terminals over which the user can gain access to the libraries and files. A greater number of users, more expertise in using the computer, but relatively fewer controllers. Another possible temporary solution is a better mix of small local computers and large time-shared central computers, with the local computer also acting as a terminal to the large central one. What you cannot do over your small local one, you transmit to the big centre.

This is fine for business, but what of the larger social systems? Look at systems like the California law enforcement computer system. Nowadays if you are stopped on a routine traffic check, some patrol car terminals can input your number to a central computer, which may instantly reply that your bank is overdrawn, and that you were once guilty of student misbehaviour of a political nature. Need we say that the systems architects of our new computer-based world should have education in the humanities?

It is worth thinking about before the whole of the known and quantitative part of the world's control system is programmed. The subject of computers is buried in myths and technical jargon. Much of it is funny, and some of it downright absurd; some of it, on the other hand, is quite blood-chilling. We will end on such a note.